Seven Cardinal Virtues in
Attaining Self-Discipline

1. Dedication (A decision)
2. Motivation (A commitment)
3. Willpower (The desire)
4. Persistence (The application)
5. Consistence (Being steady, habitual)
6. Patience (Attaining acceptance)
7. Expectancy (Maintaining faith)

Then through trials, troubles, tribulations, one arrives at the best things in life, and the trials are forgotten.

By the Same Author

EDGAR CAYCE'S STORY OF JESUS

EDGAR CAYCE'S

STORY OF

ATTITUDES

AND

EMOTIONS

Jeffrey Furst

A BERKLEY MEDALLION BOOK
published by
BERKLEY PUBLISHING CORPORATION

For my parents who accepted me as I was

CONTENTS

Introduction

". . . we are the combined result of what we have done (individually and in groups) about the ideals we have set."
1549-1

Students of the Edgar Cayce psychic data will recognize this statement as one of the philosophical principles repeatedly emphasized throughout the 14,000 psychic readings which he gave over a period of forty-three years for thousands of different people. The spiritual nature of man, or soul, is conceived of as a unit of energy created by God eons prior to earth's creation "to help bring creation to flower." Our souls, in a series of incarnations as men in the earth, build through their choices (free will) their total condition of body and mind at any given point in expression. Our attitudes and emotions clearly reflect our state of being. They offer not only ways of reviewing growth patterns, but also a way of measuring thoughts, words, and actions in the light of universal laws, thus enabling us to produce a more creative, spiritually focused life experience.

In this book Jeffrey Furst has pulled together pertinent data from the Edgar Cayce files on basic attitudes toward sex, religion, health, particular races, families, and such emotions as fear, anger, hate, joy, courage, love, gentleness, etc.

Mr. Furst's treatment is not just a cataloguing of Edgar Cayce statements. It is a selection and arrangement of extracts, with comments, suggesting ways of strengthening one's own constructive attitudes and emotions and directing and controlling the negative. His comments are brief, perceptive, and helpful.

The author raises three age-old questions which we

have all asked ourselves at one time or another: "Who am I?" "Why am I here?" "Where am I going?" With the help of the Edgar Cayce readings, Jeffrey Furst has dealt directly with the second of these and in so doing has suggested thought-provoking answers to the first and last.

Edgar Cayce's Story of Attitudes & Emotions is a workbook concerned with self-understanding, self-examination, self-reconstruction, and, paradoxically, finally, self-elimination.

It is strong medicine, but the time for strong medicine may well be here—and there seem to be people around, especially young people, who are ready to try it.

HUGH LYNN CAYCE

Acknowledgments

Our deepest appreciation is extended to the many individuals and sources of information that have contributed to this volume of thoughts and concepts. In reality everyone I've ever met or whose works I've read has added some part of himself to this, for I am to no small degree what they have given me as food for thought and becoming. In turn, these efforts of mine will now become part of the reader in whatever way one desires to regard them—which is basic to how our attitudes and emotional responses work within and through us.

Special recognition goes to Gladys Davis Turner and Mae Gimbert St. Clair for their many years of indexing, catologing and extracting much of the Edgar Cayce materials that I've quoted from—and to the many A.R.E. people who carry on this commendable work. To the following whose works we have quoted from:

Mr. Lewis Mortenson and W. Lindsay Jacob, M.D.

Mrs. Pitirim A. Sorokin for her late husband's *Forms and Techniques of Altruistic and Spiritual Growth.*

Holt, Rinehart and Winston for Thomas Sugrue's *Stranger in the Earth.*

To all my students—who taught me far more than I ever taught them. To Genevieve, my faithful helpmeet and typist, who has shared the birth pangs and joys of three books based on the Edgar Cayce materials.

And finally, to Hugh Lynn Cayce, who has shared much of his time and experience with these concepts in shaping our final manuscript.

Foreword
"The Two-Edged Sword"

(From the Cayce Readings)*

"As He hath given, *"I came not to bring peace but a sword."* I came to *give* peace, not as the world counts peace—but as that which makes for the experiences wherein the soul, the entity, is to *fulfill* those purposes, those activities, for which it—the soul-entity—came into being." (854-4)

And yet as He gave, "I came not to bring peace but to set as naught those who cherish the thought of self-exaltation, self-glory, self-aggrandizement, and to set father against son and mother against daughter, and home against house!" Why? For the very same reasons that self-aggrandizement, self-indulgence creates and builds—that which makes for avarice, hate, anger, and madness in the experiences of all who follow in that way.

But to those who have chosen the more excellent way—ye have seen, ye have known, "As ye do it unto the least of these, my brethren, ye do it unto thy Maker."

And *again* ye have seen, when to man's estate—alone on the Cross, yea into the grave, all hope seemed abandoned; yet even as the Inn could not contain His birth, neither could the Grave contain His body—because of IT *being purified* in love, in service, in harmony to God's Will. "For not of myself," said He, "but the Father that worketh in and through me do I bring thee health, do I bring thee hope, do I bring thee the *living waters.*" (1152-4)

* Most of the italics for emphasis (and explanation in parentheses within the readings) are mine. J.F.

11

The biblical reference to Jesus' statement of "coming not to send peace, but a sword" (Matt. 10:34) has been variously debated and interpreted through the centuries. The Edgar Cayce readings have dealt with the statement on the basis of the interplay between our individual soul purposes for coming into the earth and the exercise of free will. These soul purposes are very often at variance with man's conscious attitudes and emotions. How we react to this conflict between our inner purposes and the expression of our own free will gives us the opportunity for peace within, or a continuing warring with self—the sword cuts both ways—with our attitudes and emotions and choice of free will as the key. The reference in the above reading to "His body . . . being purified in love, in service, in harmony to God's Will" is an excellent example of this concept. (As in Gethsemane, when the Master prayed that this cup might pass and resolved it with, "But Thy will, not mine, be done.")

Any comprehensive study of the Edgar Cayce materials on attitudes and emotions must necessarily begin with the basic concept of man as a spiritual being—with mind and body serving as extensions of a spiritual being projecting into the physical creation, or Earth. This trinity of physical motions, mental attitudes, and spiritual essence is fundamental to a three-dimensional earthly existence in much the same manner as the triune of Father, Son, and Holy Spirit is relative to the One God.

In speaking of spirit and spiritual concepts one Cayce reading makes this comment concerning "Books":

To many the question arises—Are there, literally, Books? As houses built in wood; wood in its essence is what? Books in their essence are what? What is more real, the book with its printed pages, its gilt edges—or the essence of that told of in the book? Which is the more real, the love manifested in the Son, the Saviour for His brethren—or the essence of love that may be seen even in the vilest of passions? They are one! (254-68)

To this we would add, "Which is the more real: a reader of a book, a human being of muscle, bone, and skin, breathing, moving within and without, with organs pulsating, blood flowing, with sensory apparatus aware of colors, sounds, words, feeling the texture of a printed page? Is this the basic reality of existence? Or is there a greater reality of spirit that brought all flesh *and* this page, into being?" The Cayce materials affirm over and again that there is indeed a far greater reality around us than what we dimly perceive through our limited sensory apparatus. This universal spiritual reality can be conceived of as the essence of things unseen, of thoughts unknown, of mysteries unrevealed, of God.

Throughout man's history the prophets and the religious leaders, the philosophers, the mystics, and the common people too, have expressed a belief in, and a longing for, this spiritual essence of Creation—a longing for the return to our source, or Godhead. It has been said that if God hadn't existed Man would have created Him. Perhaps, as co-creators, we have. Our images of God are personal, illusory, and ever-changing. Perhaps that, too, is part of God's plan.

How, then, do these concepts relate to attitudes and emotions? According to the story of Creation as told through the Edgar Cayce readings, all souls were created at once, of Spirit—or God, much as if a great Cosmic Fire had shot off sparks, portions of self, into the physical creation of the universe. Each soul spinning through time and space was an offspring of the Creator, but without soul experience—similar to an uncut record or a blank recording tape. The soul's awareness of Creation was to be subsequently recorded within "The skeins of time and space" as "God's Book of Remembrance," often referred to as the Akashic records or the "Book of Life." Therein, no experience is ever lost; every thought, word, deed, experience, and relationship is "programmed," as it were, in the individual's unconscious memory. The soul's longing is ever to return to at-onement with the Creative Source—God—but meanwhile there are lessons to be learned and Creation to be experienced. Within our own solar system, according to the Cayce materials, we have developed our emotional bodies during many incarnations in the flesh, and our mental attributes during interim planetary experiences between our Earth lives. The lessons to be learned in the Earth experiences are determined according to an individual's Soul Purposes and Ideals and the interplay of free will throughout.

According to Cayce the Earth is a spiritual laboratory wherein we have the opportunity to "put it all together" —mentally, physically, spiritually—within the framework of our spiritual ideals and purposes, with *mind as the builder*. As a phrase, "Mind is the builder" can be found repeated hundreds of times throughout the Cayce materials. However, as a thought or concept it hangs incomplete unless we come to understand what Mind *is* and what it is that we have built or are building.

Cayce equates Mind with the Creative Force or First Cause—that which we conceive of as God. The readings state that as offspring of the Creator, we have Mind as an attribute of our individual soul, and as such we are *Co-Creators* with God. However, there are responsibilities to be shared in this Co-Creation, for we have as a birthright of the soul "Free Will," which allows the individual to err or stray from the path of Divine Law or Universal Law, and yet with understanding to return according to Karmic Laws—and it *is* God's will that we *do* return to Him. In this manner Creation is a continuing process in which we are all personally involved in accordance with the Universal Law of Karma, or cause and effect—the biblical "Eye for an eye, tooth for a tooth" concept. Or, "Who lives by the sword shall perish by the sword." For comparison we might imagine Mind as a great cosmic loom, spinning in Time—with "Will as the Weaver." Thus, as we view our individually woven swatches of fabric (soul records, past and present), there will be seen, more than likely, some areas of excellent cloth—well woven, orderly, beautifully colored and patterned—interspersed with bland spots or blotches, snags, tears, missing threads, and erratic and even chaotic designs.

In short, that which mind has built or experienced in

material consciousness is imprinted (for good or ill) with what we refer to as attitudes and emotions (positive or negative) *toward* those prior experiences. Consequently, we are continually responding to situations, geographic locations, and people, real or imagined, that we have memory of from past experiences, either in this lifetime or from others, for, "As ye sow so shall ye reap." Thus the man who has given his neighbor cause to fear or distrust him will eventually live to know fear and distrust within himself, and so he "meets self." Conversely, that which has been built in kindness, love and understanding will return to the builder in the same manner.

For mind is the builder and that which we think about may become crimes or miracles. For thoughts are things and as their currents run through the environs of an entity's experience thoughts become barriers or stepping stones, depending upon the manner in which the thoughts are laid as it were. For *as* the mental dwells upon these thoughts, so does it give strength, power to things that do not appear. And thus does indeed there become that as is so oft given, that *faith is* the evidence of things not seen. (906–3)

Within the readings there can scarcely be found an individual case where the attitudes and emotions of the entity are not considered and touched upon in detail. For along with ideals and purposes, attitudes and emotions are repeatedly given as the four-square foundation of an individual's pyramid of soul growth. And soul growth or soul development in learning to *be* God's will in the earth *is* according to the readings *the purpose* for which we incarnate and experience the earth and its surrounding environs. Thus we glorify God and creation and grow in consciousness.

Therefore, all that we are at any moment in time— physically, mentally, emotionally, spiritually—is the sum total of all we have ever been, or experienced, in our past/present awareness (or consciousness) as Co-Creators of all that exists.

Moreover, the readings stress that as individuals *we are personally, wholly responsible for what we are—physically, mentally, emotionally, spiritually*, stating, "As we are, where we are, and with whatever we have in hand." The attitude involved in just accepting this fact and picking up our own burden of responsibility is fundamental to a determined movement in the direction of spiritual growth and final attainment of our individaul Christ Consciousness (or Atonement with the Father).

Our purpose and opportunity in the earth, then, is to weave and reweave anew, with a joyful, loving awareness, those attitudes and emotions which are found hindersome or destructive to our own beings, and especially those harmful to any fellow being. Additionally, and most importantly, we are to build anew with those constructive emotions and attitudes often referred to as "The Fruits of the Spirit"—patience, kindness, longsuffering, brotherly love, etc.

As another parallel we would point, as the readings do, to Jesus who became the Christ, as *the Master* of His attitudes and emotions during His experience in the earth —and the Pattern—the Way, to which all should aspire.

In the development, then, that man be one with the Father, [it is] necessary that the soul pass—with its companion, the Will—through all the various stages of development, until the will is lost in Him, and he becomes one with the Father.

The illustration of this we find in the man called Jesus. (900–10)

For without passing through each and every stage of development, there is not the correct vibration to become one with the Father— Then in the many stages of development throughout the universe or in the great system of the universal forces, *each stage of development is made manifest in flesh—which is the testing portion of the Universal Vibration*. In this manner, then, and for this reason, all are made manifest in flesh and there is the development through aeons of time and space, called Eternity. (3744)

It is not by chance that each entity comes into the world; but rather as part of a plan, to fill a place which no other soul could fill so well. Each material manifestation is an undertaking by an entity in its attempts to become more attuned to a consciousness of God, and to glorify Him in the entity's relationships with other souls. (2533–1)

In giving the interpretations of these Akashic records, these are upon the skeins of time and space. Oh, that all would realize this and come to the consciousness that what we are is the combined result of what we have done (individually and in groups) about the ideals we have set! (1549–1)

Each entity should know that every thought and act are the material out of which they are building their very being. The sojourns in the various spheres are but the results of their own desires. (311–2)

So soon as man contemplates his free will he thinks of it as a means of doing the opposite of God's will, though he finds that only by doing God's will does he find happiness. Yet, the notion of serving God sits ill with him, for he sees it as a sacrifice of his (own) will. Only in disillusion and suffering, in time, space, and patience, does he come to the wisdom that his real will is the will of God, and in its practice is happiness and heaven. (2537)

As humans we are in the earth, yet we are not *of* the earth, and as spiritual beings, all we may know of happiness and heaven is within our own selves. Spirit then is the First Cause. The body (as the Temple of the Living God) is the result. Mind is the Builder. Thus, it follows, in our opinion, that "the two-edged sword" is the potential application of Karma or Grace within our individual existences. If we choose the path of the Master in truly *being* God's Will in the earth we come under His Grace

—and that sword's edge cuts clean, and peacefully so. But if we persist in pursuits of self—and Cayce states that *all sin is Self*—we continue on the wheel of Karma, again and again meeting attitudes and emotions which we have built in past experiences. And, as some have noted, that other edge of the sword is often rusty and ragged.

Chapter I

Attitude Is More Important Than Fact

On July 20, 1969, Astronaut Neil Armstrong emerged from a space capsule some 250,000 miles from Earth and, while millions of television viewers watched, became the first man to set foot upon the moon. Since that time other astronauts have experienced the same monumental unique experience in space, yet there are in existence today numerous relatively intelligent, otherwise normal humans who insist it never happened—that the masses have been completely deluded by some weird government hoax—a conspiracy of monumental proportions! There is even a well-publicized organization in England named "The Flat Earth Society," which seriously challenges with interesting logic all such claims of space travel and evidence that the earth is round. Fact or fancy? It doesn't really matter to the individual who believes in hoaxes or hearsay, for attitude can surmount either reality or fancy.

Appropriate to this line of thought, there is an old tale of a man who couldn't believe the earth was round and so set out to prove it to himself one way or another, once and for all. Heading in a line due west he eventually returned to the exact spot where he began. As a result he continued to believe the earth to be flat.

There is another tale of a farmer who visited a zoo and upon seeing a giraffe for the first time said, "There ain't no such animal!" Whereupon he shook his head and walked away. In many similar ways we observe that men's attitudes and opinions are often at variance with fact, fancy, or demonstrable proof. "As a man believeth, so he is," holds true here in that belief makes one's attitudes

19

more important than fact because one's attitudes *become* factual for the individual, regardless of any actuality involved. If a man thinks he is oppressed then he *is* oppressed—regardless of any condition around him. One Cayce reading on "Freedom" states:

> One may be free in thought, though the body may be bound in chains; and be much more free than those who are chained by their own consciousnesses. (1669–1)

> Live with this in mind (and every soul may take heed): YE SHALL PAY EVERY WHIT, THAT YE BREAK OF THE LAW OF THE LORD. For the law of the Lord is perfect, it converteth the soul. (However) it doesn't always convert a hard-headed man nor a body that is beset with habits that have left their mark upon those portions of the body through which mind and soul may work. (3559–1)

The indication here is that while Universal Laws are perfect, they in themselves do not convert those who are hardheaded, bigoted, shortsighted, or in error. The individual must do it himself! (Once again the element of free will.)

> Whatever a man sows . . . (and that means woman too!) that must he reap—whether in the spiritual, mental or material activities . . . but how was the principle set by the Master? "Thou has red, thou shalt do this or that, but I say unto you, it is in mind!"

> It is the attitude that counts. For one may lie just as much with a look as with words. (4038–1)

The above-mentioned principle alludes to the biblical references in the Sermon on the Mount concerning lust and adultery as being possible in mind as well as in physical actuality. But Cayce indicates that the principle given therein goes far beyond simple sex drives or sexual fantasies. A man can lust and scheme after another man's political office, his business, or his social position, and be equally as sinful as if he had committed adultery—in mind or actuality. It's all in the attitude one takes—whether one seeks to serve self, or others.

For the greater individual is the one who is the servant to all. And to conquer self is greater than taking many cities. For here ye may find humbleness as against that which cries oft for expression, and the feeling of not being appreciated. Express it more in the greater amount of love upon those who may be aided through thy effort. *For remember, man looks upon the things of the day but God looks upon the heart.* And that ye build in the minds and hearts of others grows and grows and grows. Thus, as an unheard of individual save in thine own environ, ye may move to keep the earth and the environs thereof in the realm in which He is ever mindful of His peoples. *For it is when man turns his back upon his Maker that the Maker's back is turned to him, only then.* (3253–2)

Or, again as the Master put it, "Whatsoever you do unto the least of these, thy brethern, ye do it unto me."

One example of "sowing and reaping" on a group or national scale is particularly demonstrable in these times. This nation's founding fathers established within our Constitution and Bill of Rights the fact that all men were created equal under the law (as we believe they are under God's Law). However, there were those individuals and groups who held an attitude that they were "more equal" than others and in actual practice over the years made a shambles of equality. Now, after many generations, the pendulum of retribution is swinging in scythelike fashion and the sins of our forbears are being felt throughout the land. Strife—political, social, racial, economic—is upon us as the Cayce readings predicted. Consider our current school integration problems and the resulting busing dilemma as an example.

Remember, as was given: "Behold thy brother is in thy hand! But if ye think hate, if ye think jealousy, if

ye act these in thy life, what can the harvest be?—
other than that manifested even in the experience of
Cain?" (3666-1)

Though He was their leader, their prophet, their Lord,
their Master—He signified—through the humbleness
of the act—(washing the Disciples' feet)—the attitude
to which each would come if he would know that true
relationship with his GOD, his fellowman. (5749-10)

Today, we as Americans stand justly accused before
ourselves and the nations of the world for perpetuating
a hypocritical social and political system—when within
our own country the guarantees of liberty, equality, and
justice must be strenuously petitioned for and literally
squeezed out of the existing governmental structure by
oppressed minority groups. All this has come to pass
within two hundred years in the nation that, as Edgar
Cayce observed, had stamped upon its coinage, "In God
We Trust."

The social injustices of decades will not be forgotten
and dissolved overnight, nor will the Karmic effects of
our military establishment's involvements around the
globe. Women will continue to agitate for liberation and
bigots will be bigots in all sizes, sexes, colors, religions,
and ethnic backgrounds.

The truth of the matter is that individually down deep
we rather like ourselves as we are—with all our past
prejudices, hatreds, superior/inferior feelings, bad habits, mistakes, ill tempers, etc.—because basically as individuals and groups we created ourselves, mentally and
emotionally. As such we resist change of anything other
than our superficial natures, and "like continues to at-
tract like." Perhaps most of us individually and nation-
ally are much like this person who questioned Edgar
Cayce: Question: "What is the matter with this body?"
Answer: "Hardheadedness, most." (5420-2)

The harmony and peace must be within SELF first, if
it is to be between one another. This ye know—ye will

never find harmony by finding fault with what the other does. Neither will the other (person) find harmony without considering what (each) will think, or be, or care for. (2811-3)

Using the experience of David the king as an example, what was it in his experience that caused him to be called a man after God's own heart? That he did not falter? That he did not do this or that, or be guilty of every immoral experience in the category of man's relationship? (For he did and was.) Rather was it that he was sorry, and not of the same offence twice! Well that ye pattern thy study of thyself after such a life! (5753-2)

What attitude can one take in order to change the fact of one's own consciousness, one's own errors and inadequacies? The clue, we feel, is in the Master's Last Command, when He said, "Love one another, even as I have loved thee and the Father loveth me." The readings state again and again that if only this *was lived* in the hearts and minds and actions of men the effect upon the earth and the affairs of men would be truly astounding. The major emphasis within the readings is on *personal application*—of self, with positive action *in serving others:*

Q: What is the law of Love?
A: Giving. As is given in this injunction—"Love Thy Neighbor as Thyself." As is given in the injunction, "Love the Lord thy God with all Thine Heart, Thine Soul, and Thine Body."

Remember—there is no greater (Biblical statement) than the injunction "God so loved Creation, or the World (as Mankind), as to give His only begotten Son for their redemption."

Now, if we, as individuals upon the earth plane, have all of the elementary forces that make to the bettering of life, and have not love—we are as nothing, nothing.

In many, many ways may the manifestations of the law of love be shown—but without the greater love, even as the Father giveth, even as the soul giveth, there is no understanding, and no compliance of the forces that make our latter law to this (Jesus' Last Commandment) of effect. (3744-4)

How should we practice giving? The readings begin with a basic attitude of joy.

As ye are joyous in thine activity? Look not upon the trials nor the temptations as hardship, nor as service, but rather as an act of love that ye may know that glory more and more.

Then bless ye the Lord. And know that His ways are not past finding out to those that diligently seek to know Him. Be in prayer oft. Be ye joyous in thy walks before men. For the Lord loveth cheer. See the beauty in the earth, in thy friend, in they neighbour; yea, even in those that would speak evil of thee. For as the spirit of truth moveth through thy words, through thy acts before men, it is the spirit of God. Do thy bit, even as the Lord *giveth* thee the opportunity day by day. (397-2)

Not that the life is to be made long-faced, that no joy is to enter! *Rather* be *joyous* in thy *living*, in thine associations, in thy activities, ever. For joy and happiness *beget* joy and happiness; unless the import be of a *selfish* nature. (480-20)

In summary, "attitude is more important than fact" in that attitude becomes fact—in being joyous, happy, unselfish, or whatever. And, if one's attitude is directed toward making one's will at one with the Father's Will, the result will be a joyous expression of life in the earth regardless of personal circumstances. So in beginning, try being joyous—it's contagious.

Chapter II

We Make Ourselves Sick

All illness is, according to the Cayce readings, sin. And all sin, indeed the only sin, according to the readings, is *self*. Historically, the word *sin* is derived from an Anglo-Saxon archery term meaning "off the mark." Thus, as we move in consciousness in error of God's Universal Laws or "off the mark," we act according to self purposes, self interests, self-centeredness, etc. And sooner or later we must pay the consequences.

The result of many of our immediate errors become quickly apparent according to the laws of cause and effect—overeating results in stomachache, overindulgence in alcohol gives one a hangover. However, the results of many of our more subtle errors are not so readily apparent. Our unconscious/subconscious mental/emotional bodies are extremely complicated and wily—more so than we care to contemplate—and our physical bodies with their varying deficiencies are the result, along with numerous conscious or unconscious mental/emotional conflicts.

At any given time we are the sum total of all we've ever experienced in this lifetime or in past lifetimes, and along with the personal responsibility this entails it gives us a sense of superiority at the unconscious (id) level. Each of us is unique—with all our faults, failures, talents, virtues, etc.—and the unconscious id crows to itself, "I made me the way I am! And I'm glad! I may have fallen arches, bad breath, myopic eyesight, indigestion, a foul temper, and a nasty disposition toward certain segments of the human race, but I built this unique soul vehicle and I'm proud of it!"

The higher self, or Christ Consciousness, has other ideas about those errant aspects of mind and will—with extremely interesting results and ramifications. The readings indicate that if an individual does not move within material consciousness in the earth according to his chosen soul purposes for entering into the physical plane, then the higher self, as it is attuned to the earthly physical/mental/emotional body, will literally *make war* with that aspect of its own self! Consider this reading on spiritual attunement in regard to our psychically attuned "sixth sense":

The sixth sense, as it may be termed for consideration here, partakes of the accompanying entity that is ever on guard before the throne of the Creator itself (the Christ Consciousness), and is that that may be trained or submerged, or left to its *own* initiative until it makes either war *with* self in some manner of expression—which must show itself in a material world as in disease, or temper, or that we call the blues, or the grouches, or any form that may receive either in the waking state or in the sleep state (as in nightmares) that has *enabled* the brain in its activity to become so changed or altered as to respond much in the manner as does a string tuned that vibrates to certain sound in the manner in which it is strung or played upon. (5754–1)

It is readily apparent from studying the lives of many psychically gifted individuals that most of them spend much of their lives in a continuing battle with physical/mental/emotional imbalances. The autobiographies of both Eileen Garrett and Arthur Ford express an almost morbid amount of detail about varieties of illnesses and accidents throughout their respective lives. And these two, now deceased, were considered the foremost American mediums of our century.

An apparent problem for such sensitive people is that they often pick up and take on the illnesses or pathological conditions of others they are attuned to or working with, in addition to any of their own basic problems. Consequently, it may be a mixed blessing to be gifted with psychic perception. With this in mind, the daughter of one of our psychic friends penned an appropriate epitaph for her mother's tombstone—"She's not really dead —she's just tuning in on someone else's condition."

For those of us who have few or no noticeable psychic abilities the problems of imbalances are not usually so dramatic, but they are here with us still. We may, for example, be accident prone or hospital-operation prone —in order to avoid responsibility or to gain sympathy; we may catch colds or develop headaches or habitually be tardy or forgetful so as to thwart our employers or families—all on a major or minor scale. Or we may go all the way, suicide being the ultimate act of selfishness, and set out to destroy ourselves, consciously or unconsciously, in one grand *acte fatale*, or piece by piece, year after year, physically/mentally/emotionally, and finally even spiritually over the course of numerous lives.

The saga of the soul's search for expression based on self alone is best exemplified in the Parable of the Prodigal Son. For each of us is a Prodigal Child at some relative stage of the journey, either going away from or returning to the Father's House. Many of us must fight or have fought that battle within self, the Higher Self making war on all levels, until eventually we fall literally flat on our backs, exhausted—physically/mentally/emotionally/socially/financially defeated—and cry out in anguish "Enough! Help me! Show me the way, Lord!" It is by His Grace that the candle is then lit and the Way is shown. The promises are that as we return we will never be given greater burdens than we can bear. (Also, as we seek we will never get into greater troubles or predicaments than we deserve!)

Meanwhile, the mental and emotional bodies we have built lifetime after lifetime will continually be tested until we lay down self ego, self will, and self purposefulness, and dissolve all our destructive, negative aspects of consciousness. In the process of being tested we "meet self"—that which we have built. The person who cries out, "You make me sick!" is more than likely meeting the very part of self that needs to be resolved within self— that which was built in consciousness somewhere in the past. Why else would the emotions be triggered if the mental/emotional body had not been that strongly programmed so to speak?

FEAR

Of all the negative emotions, fear is basic to an understanding of self and others. Consider when the Master chided His disciples, asking, "Why grow ye fearful, O ye of little faith?" There He was illustrating a lesson of Faith in preparation for far greater storms to come than the winds and waters of the Sea of Galilee. The readings note: "Perfect love casteth out fear. Where fear enters, there sin lieth at the door." (136–18)

What is indicated here in reference to sin—or self? Are not our recurrent fears and worries invariably centered around some aspects of self? Our modern society has ingrained in us numerous socially accepted worries and fears: fear of failure, fear of losing our health, fear of aging or dying, fear of being robbed or physically attacked, fear of strangers or people "different" from ourselves. All these pose threats to self and our immediate projections of self: possessions, family, friends or associates. Our fears if not understood or controlled will eventually destroy us: "Fear is the greatest destructive force to man's intelligence. When will is in conflict with creative energy's purpose in the earth, doubt, fear and uncertainty result." (101–1)

The results of fear to the physical body are well known in each individual's experience. Ask yourself what was it that frightened you most as a child? Or now as an adult? Did it make you physically ill? Emotionally or mentally shattered?

Through the blood supplying force we find the blood has been over-charged with those elements thrown off in the circulation by fear. (4610–1)

Fear, then, in that sense, is not well for a general physical condition of the body. But when a body, as in this
condition, adheres to the general principles; that is, if
there are good eliminations daily, sufficient exercise—
physical, mental and spiritual—and an even balance
or co-ordinant activity kept, we may live a full life
expectancy. (5233–1)

The Cayce readings are also constructive in this respect:

Know as has been given of old, the fear of the Lord is
the beginning of wisdom; but the fear of man is the
indication of weakness in the body-man. (531–9)

Undoubtedly there was a time in man's primitive
past when fear was essential to his survival. As a result,
fear of the elements, wild animals, other people, poi-
sonous fruits or berries, etc., has been programmed in
our unconscious bodies as memory or karma. Very probably our past associations with pain are imbedded there
also and help to trigger many fear responses. However,
since fear is destructive to the body it must be overcome
in order for an individual to evolve spiritually and function freely in the process.

Q: What is the cause of my fear and how may I overcome it?
A: By seeing the ridiculous and yet the funny side of
every experience. Knowing and believing in whom ye
have trusted, in the Lord; for without that consciousness of the indwelling, little may be accomplished.
Q: What is the cause of my fear?
A: Self-condemnation. (5302–1)

Q: How can I overcome fear of advancing old age and
being alone?
A: By going out and doing something for somebody
else! That is, those not able to do for themselves—making others happy, forgetting self entirely. These are as

material manifestations but in helping someone else you'll get rid of your feelings. (5226-1)

If one does not begin to solve the elementary problem of fear his next emotional response will be anger.

For fear creates anger. (5735-1)

Anger causes poisons to be secreted by the glands (adrenals principally). Joy has the opposite effect. (All the glands are involved to some extent.) (281-54)

The readings place a continual emphasis on seven spiritual centers of the body which are closely associated with major endocrine glands. (Eastern philosophies refer to these as "Chakras.") They are said to function as contacts or relay points between our spiritual body and the manifested physical body as it expresses itself in flesh, mind and emotion. The seven glands are: the pituitary, pineal, thyroid, thymus, adrenals, Cells of Leydig (Lyden) and Gonads. For a more lengthy description, consult the A.R.E. publications, *Meditation Gateway to Light* and *Commentary on the Book—The Revelation* (of John).

Never take food, meat or drink, when worried in mind, physically tired, or mad. . . .

Never think that either worry or madness may be drowned in drink or in overfeeding the stomach; for these bring distresses to the body. (4124-1)

For just as hate and animosity and hard sayings create poisons in the body, so do they weaken and wreck the mind of those who indulge in same . . . and then they begin to wonder why this or that has befallen me. . . . (1315-10)

Do not belittle, do not hate. For hate creates as does love, and brings turmoils and strifes. (1537-1)

Among the daughters of Zerubbabel—*the entity swore vengeance. And he who swears vengeance pays*—even to the last farthing. (5177–1)

Remember, vengeance belongeth to the Lord and not to an individual human. For individuals in the earth are prone to allow selfishness to control. (4038–1)

The readings pointed out many times over that a person could not hold hatred and anger toward his fellowman without eventually coming down with heart, stomach, and/or liver problems: "To be sure the attitudes oft influence the physical conditions of the body. No one can hate his neighbor and not have stomach or liver trouble. One cannot be jealous and allow anger of same and not have upset digestion or heart disorder." (4021–1)

The fact that stress, tension, or anger would often cause stomach ulcers, gall bladder attacks, or heart palpitations was well known years before the term "psychosomatic illness" was introduced as a modern catchall both within and outside the medical profession. The Cayce readings gave credence to psychosomatic conditions beginning with Edgar's very first readings on himself some seventy years ago. His own throat paralysis and inability to speak literally pushed him into giving psychic readings for himself and eventually many others, many of whose conditions he described as psychosomatic in nature—that is, a physical disorder resulting from an emotional or mental cause, often with its roots extending into past life experiences.

In the classic medical examples such patients are found to have nothing physically wrong with them. The patient may be having considerable pain or discomfort, or even be totally blind or paralyzed, but medical diagnosis finds that there is nothing organically wrong with him. Here we are reminded again of "Attitudes being more important than Fact" with "Mind as the Builder." The person who is hysterically blind or paralyzed is just as sightless or immobile as someone with a severed spinal

cord or injured optic nerves. However the inner consciousness contains the key to cause and motive. Each
pain itself and one's attitude toward it seems to be en-
meshed in one's karmic body (as memory), going back
many, many lifetimes.

Our point is that apparently most of humanity's ills
are far more deeply seated than we've previously credited
them with being—and many chronic hypochondriacs may
have some justification for their complaints. They really
are ill! However, this does not excuse any one of us for
not attempting to be the healthiest possible expression of
the Creative Force in the earth. The Karmic ramifications, for good or ill, are infinite.

Q: Will surgery be advisable for the liver?
A: Not if the applications suggested are made and as
the attitude is changed. If the body continues to hold
onto and enjoy being worked on by the doctors, put
on by same, pulled and hauled about by others—well,
you might as well keep on doing it!

But we have indicated how to meet the condition—
first within self, *quite feeling sorry for self!* Do something about it that will be constructive, by doing
something for others as well—by being more quiet.
(3574-1)

Here we have an unbalanced condition in the nerve
system, in the assimilating system, in the glandular
system; yet *the body attempts*—through the activity of
the Creative forces in all three of these systems—*to
ADJUST itself TO the disturbances;* and to do the
best it can with what it has! *If we would only attempt
to do that in our own minds,* how much happier the
world would be! (1709-1)

Ye are sensitive to things about you; because ye have
lived not only in the experience but in many others in
a very EXTRAVAGANT life in EVERY phase of your
association with your fellowman.

Have ye not found within—as in thine own body in the present—that the extravagance of thy living has produced those very inclinations that arise in thy digestive forces? Thus thy high blood pressure . . . arises from this overindulgence, this activity. And unless ye make reparation, these conditions will overcome thee!

As to the material activities—keep away from those things that HINDER—such as the effects of alcohol, of riotous living, of indulgences in great quantities of stimulations. . . . Or, as just given be CONSIST-ENT! (1537–1)

For the entity pities self. And an individual soul that begins to pity self soon finds fault with others and forgets the real freedom. (2706–1)

But if there is the constant resistance kept as through the holding of resentments, the creating of activities in the finding of fault here and there, we will continue to have a reaction that will be a very nervous, a very disturbing physical as well as mental-material condition. (1819–1)

And keep the constructive mental attitude. Never resentments, for this naturally creates within the system those secretions that are hard upon any circulation, and especially where there is disturbance with the spleen, the pancreas, and a portion of the liver activity. (420–19)

Q: What debt do I owe John Martin?
A: Only that ye build in thine own consciousness. For every soul, as every tub, must sit upon its own bottom. *And the soul that holds resentment owes the soul to whom it is held, much!* Hast thou forgiven him the wrong done thee? Then thou owest him naught! (1298–1)

Here is an interesting spiritual truth. (1298–1) That according to the readings if I am wronged and subsequently hold resentment, then I am the one at fault! I am the one who loses, and I owe the one who wronged me much! Conversely, if I truly forgive, then I owe nothing—and, additionally the readings note as we forgive we become masters over those we've forgiven!

To a great degree, this is part of the beauty of the Cayce materials. Whereas they were given for other individuals, very often some of the specific readings seem to jump out just for us. Consider this reading which was given for a drug addict, but is applicable to anyone's deeply ingrained habit formations.

There are evidences of a weakness in the *physical* body through the desire for GRATIFYING of appetite that has blocked the will of the mental forces (by gratifying a physical desire for the emotions of a mental and physical experience) thus becoming a destructive influence to the physical and mental body. . . . In the gratifying of a desire, these become habit-forming; in the manner of the effect then of the drug, and the effects of alcohol upon the system, weakening the will and thus weakening the coordination between the manifestations of spiritual truth with material gratification of flesh desires. (1427–1)

Q: Is cigarette smoking injurious to me, and how can I break the habit?
A: Make up your mind that you'll quit! This is not injurious, done in moderation. But as indicated, in most everything this body does it is all out of proportion. (3258)

Many readings noted that moderate cigarette smoking was not harmful. But these statements were made for specific individuals, and long before the current methods of tobacco spraying and chemical treatment were introduced. Today even moderation is questionable in our opinion, although some individual psychological factors may override total abstinence.

Along with fear, anger and resentment, it has often been stated that hate is the opposite of love, but this is not necessarily the exact relationship. One of our most respected friends is a psychiatrist—Dr. W. Lindsay Jacob of Pittsburgh, Pennsylvania—who is as well versed in the Cayce materials as he is in his own profession. He shares the opinion, along with many colleagues, that the opposite pole to hatred is *desire*, rather than love. In turn the opposite to true love is total apathy or indifference. The Cayce materials affirm that we can only hate that which we've once loved. They are very close to one another.

Q: Psychoanalytically speaking, does the entity have a split personality?
A: It has split desire rather than personality! The individual lacks stability, with the individuality being stabilized in an ideal that takes hold upon the infinite. The possibilities of the entity are unlimited, but self gets in the way and becomes the stumbling block. (4083–1)

Between desire and apathy we find pessimism:

In giving the interpretation of the record, there is much to choose from—and while that which may be given here may appear as condemning, this takes not from the latent and the manifested abilities which are manifested in this entity; there are those tendencies for this entity to see only the dark side of any experience. The entity is pessimistic as to the outcome of any venture. (5302–1)

The eternal pessimist is very often motivated by self-failure or need for self attention. How often have we heard the prideful expression, "Oh, *I'm the world's worst!*" (At this, that or the other.) Such crowings of course ultimately take the form of an ego trip.

There is a tendency ever in the physical body, in this as well as in any other, when the mind and the body are not kept active, to revert to pessimism. (642-2)

And finally, apathy:

As to the Nerve System, here we find a sympathic condition. For, with the aggravations to the mental body, these are as periods when the body—as it were—does not *care! And woe to all those that reach that attitude,* whether in their mental bodies or in their physical bodies, for *some portion must suffer from a "don't care" attitude,* either mentally or physically, or both. (530-1)

The end-all here of course is insanity. Dr. Lindsay Jacob has defined insanity as a state of being in which an individual is unable to consider any thought, viewpoint, or action other than his own. The final sin or selfishness, then, is insanity, suicide, or both. So in the end there is no exit from self—other than the Way shown by the Master: "Remember the injunction—Never worry as long as you can pray. When you can't pray, you'd better begin to worry! For then you have something to worry about!" (3569-1)

Chapter III

Four Aspects of Mental/Emotional Growth

During eight of the past twenty-two years I have been a secondary school teacher—in Ohio, New York City, and Virginia—teaching biology, science, health, physical education, and coaching athletics. Along the way I experienced other diverse experiences in sales, advertising, writing, and editing. Yet, in all the years and in all the fields of endeavor I was continually struck by some basic awareness I'd picked up in college, in an evolution/anthropology class in which the professor, Dr. William Shideler, posed the problems of theory regarding evolution and society from the classic standpoint—of inherited genetic characteristics versus environment—and left the conclusions to us. Perhaps his wisdom in allowing his students the choice was the very point he wished to make, for in the final analysis neither heredity nor environment can stand up against an individual's or a group's choice of Free Will, attitudes, and desires.

Throughout history, with properly motivated desires, attitudes, and will, battles have been fought and won, athletic victories attained—tremendous sacrifices made —happily and willingly despite any or all portents of defeat. Whether in athletics, warfare, or individual attainment the crucial impetus upon the balance scale has been Man's Will—the birthright of the soul accordng to Edgar Cayce.

Now some twenty-five years later, our psychologists and sociologists have been sounding the alarm that we, as individuals and as a nation, are suffering from a loss of purpose and will—a loss of identity as it were—far removed from the ideals, purposes, and attitudes which our Founding Fathers had formulated in constructing the basis for our society only two hundred years ago.

Edgar Cayce stated in his readings that this nation must either continue that role in the earth to which our fore-fathers had dedicated themselves or the mantle of world leadership would wend its way westward to the Orient. Thus, this problem of identity (and purpose) can relate to groups and nations as well as for individuals. The problem has been well summed up by these four questions—

WHO AM I?
WHY AM I HERE?
WHERE DID I COME FROM?
WHERE AM I GOING?

These questions are not easily answered by any nation or individual. However, we would offer the opinion that no man in history had a better answer to these or was more aware of His identity than Jesus of Nazareth. Here was a man who knew *who* He was—*why* He was here—where He had come from—and where He was going.

In following Him, as did Edgar Cayce (both asleep and awake), we can begin to solve this problem of identity for individuals, groups, and even nations—if only we apply His last commandment, "That we love one an-other."

This, of course, is again our choice. But along with choice and free will Professor Shideler added the follow-ing framework for all considerations of attitudes and their resultant emotional responses. All forms of mental health and social behavior fit neatly within these four confines and serve as a basis for self-understanding. The Cayce materials have further reinforced my long-held views on these attitudes and the importance of our analyzing such viewpoints from an individual standpoint.

The four aspects are:

1. ATTITUDES TOWARD SELF.
2. ATTITUDES TOWARD OTHERS.
3. ATTITUDES CONCERNING SEX AND SEX-
   UALITY (both as regards self and others).
4. ATTITUDES CONCERNING RELIGION/ETH-
   ICS-MORALITY (again as regards both self and
   others).

An entire volume could be written on any one of
these and *we strongly recommend that such be done—
by you, the reader, as author!*

The Cayce materials continually gave advice from a
practical standpoint regarding the application of information given. That is, if you could apply such advice in your own life, in your associations with your
fellowman, then you were admonished to do it. "Either
accept or reject" is a standard notation throughout the
readings, and individuals were often finally told to *do
something—even if it was wrong!* For only through
action and movement in consciousness can we test
what we hold to be our ideals and purposes. The re-
cipients of Cayce readings were told to write down
their ideals—aligining them in columns of Mental/
Emotional/Physical/Spiritual. (To these we suggest
you add Material Surroundings/Work or Profession/
Geographical Locations.) This written exercise is basic to the Study Group Program carried on throughout the country within the ARE. The groups use as
a handbook the practical advice given to an initial
group of Edgar Cayce's friends. Titled *A Search for
God*, its two volumes contain instructional information on "How to Meditate," "How to Pray," and practical lessons on such subjects as "Cooperation," "Patience," "Love," "Knowing Self," and many others.
(All of this seems very simple and easy—until you attempt to *apply it* in your own life!)

To know self is thus basic, and the beginning of all
personal philosophy and wisdom. Yet how many of us
truly know self? An initial step, as we've suggested, is

to write your own book, for reference purposes, on what your attitudes really are, beginning with attitudes regarding self.

ATTITUDES TOWARD SELF

Few individual souls really enjoy their own companionship, not merely because they love themselves the less or that they despise themselves the more. But their thoughts and things and emotions of the body are seldom in accord one with the other—or their (unconscious) individuality and their (conscious) personality don't reflect the same shadow in the mirror of life. (3351-1)

Ask yourself, do you really like *you*—as a person, as a friend, as a confidant? Would you like to have another person just like yourself around you in whatever association you care to choose—spouse, relative, business associate, social companion, parent, child, teacher, student, roommate, lover, fellow explorer? Would you have a friend you could trust, admire, take most anywhere, count upon when the going got difficult? Would you be able to communicate with such a person easily, both verbally and nonverbally? Would that other person be aware and considerate of all levels of your personal past/present/future and would he have a life-style that was constructive, creative, or exciting? Would he be "groovy" or a "drag"? Add your own questions, ad infinitum. You'll likely find, as almost all of us do, that our ideal-projected self falls somewhere short of what we truly are at present. But that's all right, we *can* change if we *desire* to!

The next question is—can you stand your own company, alone, with just your own thoughts for any length of time? Have you ever tried it? For how long? Could you go off into the woods for months as Thoreau and others have done and be content with being still and alone? "The entity finds that there are periods when it likes to be alone. And fortunate indeed is the entity who has applied or may so apply self as to find self good company." (1664–2)

Most people do not find themselves to be satisfactory company for very long, man being essentially a social creature. If when alone, one immediately has to turn on the radio or TV, or be on the telephone, then we have food for thought! Or if food is your crutch then the refrigerator or the liquor cabinet will beckon most often. How do *you* relate to loneliness?

Also, ask yourself—what are your worst habits or tendencies? Are they worth changing? And if not are you going to learn to accept them, modify them, or let them gnaw away at you from now on? In a later chapter we'll discuss balanced living and the importance of positive attitudes regarding a healthy body, mind, and life-style. But for now, ask yourself, if you were to have a child (or if you have a child now) what personal attributes do you have (physically/mentally/emotionally/morally) that you would prefer your child didn't have? By the same token consider those elements about yourself that in all fairness you admire, all your positive attributes—intelligence, fairness, judgment, kindness, etc. Which of these—any or all—would you wish to pass on to your child?

NOW CONSIDER THIS. If we are at present the sum total of all we've been before, both in this lifetime and times past, *does it not follow that at present, and for the rest of this lifetime, we are individually creating the child that we will be the next time around?* In short—WE ARE OUR OWN CHILD! Say to yourself, "I AM MY OWN CHILD, and am now creating that which I shall become—good, bad or indifferent—and that choice is mine alone!"

Therefore, as we've noted before, from the standpoint of the Cayce materials, it is no excuse to blame Mom or Dad or society or our immediate associates for what we are now, or are to become. All our positive attributes are recorded on God's side of the ledger. The negative shortcomings belong to self and are listed in the debit columns. It is for us to balance our accounts and wipe out the old debts. *But first we must know self.*

As a small child I used to get angry with my parents and run around the house wailing, "I didn't ask to be born!" But the Cayce readings note, "Oh, yes you did!" *We choose our parents before birth.* We chose our sex, nationality, race, place of birth, and knew pretty well what channels in life we should pursue. (And if we don't pursue them as intended, things seem wrong—we live under a cloud.)

I should note here that these choices are not very simple and apparent to our present conscious minds. Many factors are involved. Recurring questions arise concerning the mechanics of how *"each soul enters to fill a role that no other soul could fill so well"* as the readings have described it. Perhaps we should liken the entire operation to a great cosmic computer, with individual soul's attributes programmed into the computer's memory banks. When an opportunity occurs for a soul to enter the earth (a pregnancy) the computer is scanned for all the souls who have a desire or need to return. Also the parents' attributes are considered at the same time along with past life associations, etc. The ideal soul is then selected to come into the situation—and out of the computer pops your card!

Although we often consciously resist or even resent our purposes for coming into the earth we know from within how best we should express ourselves in this life, and this we can and will know if only we allow ourselves to *be* God's will in the earth. So if you haven't already done so, learn to express yourself, for *expression is the essence of existence.* At the same time one's expressions should be meaningful, for *meaningful expression is* (and note here that we consider meaningful expression as the ability to communicate truly with self and others) *the essence of being truly alive.* Or, as one musician/poet has put it, "Love God—and let your whole instrument wail!"

Too long has the entity been, as it were, under a cloud; rather timid, rather lacking in self-expression. It needs to get out in the wilds and yell, and hear its own echo back again! (Holler, yell more, for the fun of it!) The body has wanted to many times and never has to the full extent in its whole experience.

The entity is not to be subdued by others who try, or have tried to impress the entity with their importance. For God is not a respecter of persons. And anyone can act the fool by appearing to be important. (3564-2)

The balance between expression, self-realization, esteem, egoism, and humility is sometimes a delicate consideration. The readings noted that we should be honest with self, yet not harsh or self-condemning. At the same time we should be careful of spiritual pride or self-exaltation.

Knowledge is well, and understanding is good; but to use these in a manner in which self—the own ego—is to be exalted, makes for confusion to those who would seek to know their place in the activities of the realms of opportunity that is given in the present. (1599-1)

It is well to be humble—and every soul should learn the lesson of being humble—but know in WHOM as well as in WHAT ye believe! Know the author of that ye would present to thy fellowman in regard to THEIR preparations for their living, their experiencing the associations, with their fellowman. For the body finds self a physical being, with a body physical, a body mental, and the hopes for—yea, the vision of—the soul.

Then, *choose thou that which is thy ideal*. Know there is set before thee today good and evil, life and death. This is the natural state of man, as a seeking soul encased in matter; but with the mind—yea, with the will —that IS eternal, and is godlike. (2031-1)

Study, yes, give expression, yes: but know there are others who are also an expression of good in the earth besides self. (5358-1)

ATTITUDES TOWARD OTHERS

With this line, as one sees the manifestations of the
acts of man in the earth, men claiming God as the
Father, the Christ as the elder brother, the patriarchs
as teachers and directors, and yet find fault with someone less gifted with the light of His Love—suppose,
for the moment, that God looked upon thine own
heart as thou hast oft looked upon thine brother's life?
—*Oblivion*, incomparable to the mind even of man—
even of space or time. (254–68)

The Master faced the crowd and challenged them
with the single statement, "He among you who is without sin, let him cast the first stone." As we know the
woman was left untouched—and yet how often still are
we inclined to find fault with others? *Ae we do find fault,
others will find fault with us.* This is the law, and the
fault is our own.

Still, among the many games people play, fault-finding
is one of man's favorites. After all, in this way we bolster
our own egos and attain a degree of mistaken spiritual
upmanship—but for a price. This is not to assume that
others are without fault or blameless and that such errors
or flaws should be passed off totally without notice. During my many years in the classroom and on the practice
field, both as teacher and as coach, it was my responsibility to point out faults and errors to students and
players. The example here is of the proper relationship,
plus the spirit of constructive criticism needed under the
circumstances. Additionally, students have tacitly agreed
that their faults should be made known to them throughout their schooling, so that they can correct themselves
and grow in the process. (There is a parallel relationship
going on between us and God, but all too often we
haven't fully realized it as yet.)

There is always some danger for the leader, teacher,
coach, or critic, however. If we use such a position for
self-aggrandizement, to feed a need for power, fame or

fortune, then we have missed the mark and we lose. The same holds true in nearly every form of relationship with others.

As noted elsewhere, the Cayce materials consistently gave credence to the problems of psychological projection—in seeing within other individual's personalities and actions one's own fears, doubts, negativity, etc.

As a man soweth, so shall he reap. As an attitude is held towards another, that is gradually builded within self. (451–1)

Hence the urge, as it were, to hold what would be called malice, and ever determining within self, "I'll get even with you yet," doesn't pay! For this only builds into self that held in thought—for thoughts are things, and become crimes or miracles! (2071–1)

. . . Then do not find fault. Rather make thine self at one with the divine within, that it (the Divine) may shine out through every act, every thought, of the body-mind; for thoughts are deeds, and may become miracles or crimes!

. . . Do not condemn self or others, for that which is past, that which cannot be rectified, is but to heap reproach upon self. . . . (5469–1)

Find less fault with others, and others will find less fault with thee. (3160–2)

Now, ask yourself, "What is my attitude about other people? What are my likes and dislikes?" List the five races and what you feel about them from firsthand experience. Do you have any strong prejudices among them? List a number of nationalities and religions and how you feel about them. What do you like or dislike about the opposite sex? Your own sex? The "other" generation? How do you feel about politicians, government workers, clergymen? Your neighbors, relatives, repairmen, teen-agers? Policemen, waiters, movie actors, TV personalities, store clerks? Your parents, your children, professional athletes, clothing designers, stockbrokers? Farmers, lawyers, business associates? (Add to your list whoever else comes to mind.) You might also ask yourself, "How do I react to individuals who are crippled, deformed, or mentally retarded?"

> Have ye looked upon the circumstances of others and envied them, coveted their position or their place? Then know ye have brought condemnation to thine own self. (1759-1)

> Then let not the green-eyed monster, jealousy, be at the root of thy troubles. (5030-1)

Envy, jealousy, covetousness, and their extreme reverse, revulsion, are among the many age-old problems which must be met if we are to grow spiritually. Again let us remember that we are no closer to the Kingdom of Heaven than our ability to love the one who has hurt us most, or who has despised us most—or we them.

In this reading Cayce paraphrases a line from Hamlet:

> To thine own self in these relationships be true—and thou wilt not be false to any. *Rather* know ye that the Lord loveth rather that of love than sacrifice; rather the purposes, the desires! *What* is thy desire toward thy fellowman? What is that motivating thy activities? Let the love of the Father *constrain* thee! (694-2)

In another reading he poses an interesting commentary on love related to tolerance:

> In Jupiter we find the universality, the ability of being tolerant. So few souls or entities have combined love in the material plane with tolerance! For, *love in the material plane becomes egotistical,* and this is the opposite of tolerance.

> For, as indicated, the ability for the application of love as related to tolerance is the greater virtue in the entity's present experience. (2629-1)

Next we would suggest you write down two columns of attitudes, emotions, and behavior—one positive, one negative—and list other people or groups that you know, according to your present attitudes regarding them. Whom do you know who would serve as a good example in each case?

Tolerant	Intolerant
Accepts errors, failures	Blames others, seldom completes difficult tasks
Self-starter	Has to be coaxed or driven
Finds some good in others	Gossips maliciously
Converses positively	Chronic complainer
Punctual	Always late
Open-minded	Opionated
Polite	Outspoken, boorish, brutal
Listens and talks intelligently	Talks but doesn't listen
Alert and to the point	Vague and illogical
Cooperates with others	Domineering, willful, or piggish
Doesn't swear around the preacher	Uses coarse language
Dependable	Shirks responsibility
Does not judge other's actions or motives	Suspicious and cynical
Self-reliant, trusting	Timid, fearful around people
Shows inner courage	Many fears, phobias
Shows consideration	Inconsiderate or abuses others
Makes allowances when needed	Inflexible
Kind and appreciative	Discourteous to underlings
Organized—plans well	Disorganized
Times movements efficiently	Wastes time
Likes outdoor activities, nature	Attached to home and furnishings

Enjoys youngsters	Dislikes children, young people
Affectionate	Cold, touchy
Controls emotions	Easily flustered or shaken
Accepts criticism	Loses temper and blames others
Gives God credit	Self-righteous or spiritually arrogant
Mentally alert/aware	Can never locate personal belongings
Shares others' accomplishments	Deflates others
Humorous, able to laugh at self	Lacks sense of humor
Controls choices	Indecisive about money
Not attached to possessions, shares	Materialistic, hoards possessions, avaricious
Honest with self, evaluates intelligently	Rationalizes
Reasonable	Unreasonable
Accepts self	Feels inadequate
Feels protected	Frightens easily
Patient	Impatient, easily frustrated
Open and honest	Secretive or deceptive to others
Modest, unpretentious	Ostentatious
Consistent, disciplined	Careless, lazy, unpunctual, breaks promises, vacillates
Happy and cheerful	Glum and grouchy
Optimistic	Apprehensive, negative
Healthy, uncomplaining	Chronically ill, hypochondriac
Creative, imaginative	Narrow-minded, helpless
Trusts in God and His guidance	Worries continually
Considers others	Cold and ruthless
Shrugs off slights	Feelings easily hurt

Open, fair, and just	Plays politics, shows favoritism
Social, friendly, thinks of others	Loner, withdraws, does not relate well to others
Outgoing, enthusiastic, playful	Depressed, moody, negative
Makes peace	Precipitates quarrels
Relaxed	Carries the burdens of the world
Forgives oppressors	Vengeful, collects injustices
Conciliatory, forgives	Holds grudges, resentments
Prays for others	Prays only for self
Prays and meditates daily for understanding and guidance	Prays or meditates only when in trouble
Intelligent	Dull, doesn't relate to consequences

After placing others on the list, where do you see yourself? Or where would others place you? It works both ways of course, for as previously noted the Cayce materials insist that the way you look at others reflects to no small degree the way you truly view yourself on the inner levels of consciousness. At first glance this seems preposterous. We say, "That couldn't possibly be me! That fault is *not mine.* I'm not that way at all!" But time seems to displace our past and present flaws, disguising them to a degree where we can stand ourselves. For if all our past errors of character were allowed to express themselves at once, in this lifetime, the effect more than likely would be shattering and insurmountable for most of us.

Then too, have you ever noticed how the people who are most inconsiderate or callous toward others are the first ones to react to any personal slights made to themselves? Or how someone who monopolizes any conversation he becomes part of usually becomes highly incensed

at whoever else does the very same thing? Or how someone who is relatively authoritative on a given subject
reacts when another person expounds on that subject in
his presence?

One of my own pet peeves has to do with politicians
and self-proclaimed "public servants" in general. (One
of my observations has been that those who loudly pro-
claim their years of service to the public often retire
from office as rather wealthy men.) I've aired my problem
of attitude toward politicians as an example during lectures around the country, and recently one lady accused
me of being anti-Republican. However, I assured her
that this was not the case. It is just that the current administration is Republican. Four years ago I sounded
very anti-Democrat!

As a Libran I tend to be expansive and fair to all. My
prejudices toward politicians are held without regard to
race, creed, sex, national origin, or political party.

My reason for bringing this up is that at present, ab-
horring politics in general, I have absolutley no desire to
run for any political office or lend myself to campaign for
anyone else. This leads me to the personal conclusion
that in past lives I've been involved in a large amount of
political maneuvering and intrigue of sorts—and I've
had quite enough. At the same time I continually recognize such activity on the part of others—with painful
awareness and a certain amount of humor I might add.
Perhaps this personal tale can provide our readers with
a key to opening clues into their own past involvements.

ATTITUDES CONCERNING SEX AND SEXUALITY

Probably no area of human awareness causes more
emotional trauma within self and in relationships with
others than sexual identity and interrelationships developed throughout various lifetimes, the present one
included. The influences on mental/emotional stability
are quite obvious and well documented elsewhere.

Here for personal observation and self-analysis are a number of items related to sexuality and sexual relationships. How the reader responds to these with initial emotional reactions or mental associations will reflect to no small degree "where he is at" regarding sexual attitudes. (Or if you'd prefer to avoid thinking about anything involved with sex, or specific items on the list, perhaps that in itself will offer a clue!) It is suggested that eventually the reader sit down with self or with some intimate friend and openly discuss what you really think and feel about many of these areas, for the attitudes involved are extremely important in human relationships.

At this point we also suggest that the subject of humor be added, possibly because there is no better area to regard humor itself than in tales or foibles about sex. And, how one laughs and what one laughs at can also be deeply revealing of self and others.

To begin, do you agree or disagree with this statement? "The most erotic part of the human body is the mind!" (If you are uncertain about it, think on it for a while!)

An appropriate story is the old one of the man who consulted a psychiatrist because people kept insisting he was oversexed. The doctor began his examination, drawing very simple figures and asking for the patient's reactions or thought associations. All such elementary figures as circles, triangles, squares; numbers one, two, three; balls, boxes, cats, dogs, horses, automobiles, beds, tables, chairs, etc., brought the patient's drooling response that they reminded him of various aspects of sex with appropriate lurid explanations of course. After this had continued for some time the doctor sat back thoughtfully and said, "You know, you really *are* oversexed." To which the patient protested, "What do you mean *me* oversexed. *You're* the one who's been drawing all the dirty pictures!" (Or, if one of the figures mentioned didn't seem sexy to you, then you are *not* oversexed.)

Once again, sex, like beauty or obscenity, is still in the eye of the beholder. Likewise, consider those individuals who protest their role of being regarded as mere sex objects—after spending much time in fashion shops, beauty parlors, cosmetic bars and in front of their mirrors. Are these not entities "meeting themselves" as the readings have put it?

QUESTIONS FOR CONSIDERATION

1. To begin, what is your present general attitude about sexual intercourse? (Note that many of the questions posed may or may not necessarily involve firsthand experience.) Do you feel that such intimacy is—(O.K. for consenting adults) (beautiful) (sinful) (for married couples only) (exciting at first, but really overrated or boring) (only to be engaged in for propagation) (disgusting) (satisfying) (detrimental to spiritual development) (spiritually fulfilling) (   )?

The Cayce readings indicate that our sexual or reproductive drives are the strongest of all basic instinctual forms of activity—that for humans to mate is as natural as the flowers to bloom. (A number of specific readings on sex are included in Chapter VI.) Indeed, the readings equate the creative or reproductive force which expresses itself in sexual activity as closely akin to the actual God force within.

Which is the more real, the love manifested in the Son, the Saviour for His brethren—or *the essence* of Love that may be seen in the vilest of passions. They are one!
Beautiful, isn't it? (254–68)

2. Have you ever considered virginity or celibacy as an ideal way of life? Virginity as more fulfilling than marriage and having children?
Humor note: Can you recall a favorite cartoon or story about same? (There are usually a few good chastity belt stories going around!)

3. Assuming you could make the choice at present, would you come back in the same sex your next lifetime? If not, why?

4. What do you find most attractive about the opposite sex—physically, mentally, emotionally? By contrast, what do you dislike or abhor sexually among them?

5. What impresses you most as being really "sexy" in the opposite sex? In your own sex? And, who, as individuals? (Both sexes.)

6. Of all the individuals you've ever known personally, who among them have aroused you to the point of really desiring to make love with them? Any one more than the rest? Can you explain to yourself why?

7. Assuming you had one last night to live and could spend it with anyone you've ever had a sexual relationship with, who would that person be? Can you explain why?

Or, if you could end it with someone with whom you've never had sexual relations, who would that be? And for what reasons?

8. If you could have a child with anyone you know, assuming all parties were free and agreeable, who would that person be? And why?

9. What is your attitude about being seen in the nude? Seeing others nude?

Humor note: Insert a favorite story.

10. How do you view your own body in regard to sexual expression—physically, mentally, emotionally? Do you feel reasonably responsive and well adjusted to other's sexuality as well as your own? (What is the funniest thing that ever happened to you in this vein?) (The most embarrassing?)

11. Have you ever felt the need for professional consultation for any personal sexual problems?

12. Do you customarily view others on the basis of their sex and how they project their sexuality?

13. Do you ever daydream about sexual fantasies or past relationships?

14. What was the content of the last erotic dream you had? And how do you regard such dreams?

15. Have you ever had a reincarnation dream about being of the opposite sex? (Many people have.)

16. What is your attitude toward the current sexual revolution: Premarital sex? The pill? Promiscuity? Legalized abortion? Venereal disease? Polygamy? Divorce? Sex education in the public schools? Pornographic or X-rated movies? Erotic literature—novels, magazines, photos? Gay Liberation—Homosexuality and Homosexuals? (Both male and female.)

17. What have your responses been to "the facts of life" from the time of first knowing the basic difference between boys and girls, and where babies really came from, in regard to: Puberty? Menstruation? Nocturnal emissions? Masturbation? Your first sexual experience? Contraceptive devices? Being examined by a doctor? Frigidity or fears of inadequacy?

Humor note: Most everyone has had some sad/funny experiences or stories to tell along these lines.

What was your honeymoon like—Happy? Sad? Funny? Tragic? No problems?

18. How do you regard the effects of aging? Menopause? Impotency? Potency?

Humor note: I've always envied the reply of an elderly gentleman who when asked how he would like to die, smiling sighed, "Shot at the age of ninety-three—by a jealous husband!"

19. In your next lifetime how would you prefer your sexuality and sex life to be? The same? If different, how?

Obviously, many of these questions are not easily resolved, but we feel that they offer food for thought and can open the doors to inner awareness where or when the individual desires to become truly more self-aware.

ATTITUDES CONCERNING RELIGION/ETHICS-MORALITY

We could very easily extend the subjects of sex and sexuality into this last area of consideration. However, we prefer not to since all too many discussions of religion and morality scarcely go beyond the original sixth Commandment which gave sex its name—sextus—"Thou shalt not commit adultery." There is even some questions of semantics regarding what originally was encompassed or not encompassed, specifically, by the term "adultery." Therefore we would prefer to concentrate here on some lesser or more subtle aspects of immorality.

To a very great extent our own personal problems of attitudes and emotions regarding morality, religion, and ethical conduct concern areas not mentioned in the Ten Commandments. It is not written that, "Thou shalt not commit obscenities." But in this world, which is the more obscene or criminal, an unfortunae degenerate who gets some form of pleasure by voicing obscenities over a telephone, or a hundred thousand Biafran children dead of starvation while, simultaneously, other nation's farmers are paid for not planting crops?

It can be pointed out historically, over and again, that one nation's obscenities are another's patriotic duties— and vice versa. Sad to say, obscenity is found in the eyes of the beholder as well as in the mouths of patriots and perverts alike. Man's inhumanity to man has been imprinted in consciousness throughout numerous lifetimes, individually and as groups or nations. It is well to keep this in mind as we attempt to understand ourselves and others.

There was no commandment that we should not sell our fellow humans as slaves, or accept them as same. Yet even today the remnants of slavery, partially disguised, still exist like a submerged iceberg, because again, as individuals and groups we have the combined past experience written within our unconscious.

Nowhere was it written that, "Thou shalt not traffic in opium, heroin, or other habit-forming drugs." But this, too, has been going on for thousands of years and is also part of humanity's unconscious.

No religious sect was ever founded that had among its fundamental tenets, "Thou shalt not engage in religious zeal or spiritual pride." And so today, as in ages past, we have thousands of fragmented groups shouting from their respective mountain tops that they alone have THE True Way, and all the rest are errant misfortunates, probably doomed to perdition, when the one True Way, the Master, gave that we should seek Oneness, within, finding common ground with all men—excluding no one —and never to attempt raising one's head above the others in sight of the Lord. He first showed this in admonishing the mother of James and John, and also in the washing of our feet—all humanity's feet—but we've forgotten these lessons at times. Even some ARE members and groups are guilty on occasion of setting themselves apart or above others in the same manner, despite what Edgar Cayce warned of again and again in the readings —that this information should not be used as the basis for a cult, sect, ism, schism, or other exclusive association.

Our intention here (and elsewhere in this chapter) is that our readers may attain a better understanding of self by becoming more aware of areas that result in strong reactions, positive or negative, regarding these basic aspects of consciousness. Consider religion. Have you ever broken off from a church affiliation? Why? Do you feel that your religion has some special tenets, truths, or an inside track to God that no other church or religious tenet has? Is there any form of doctrine or segment of doctrine that disturbs you in your church or others? Have you married, or ever considered marrying, someone of another religious faith? Did it cause personal problems, or problems within either family? What of any children born within a mixed marriage? What is your attitude regarding prayer in the public schools? Should Roman Catholic priests be allowed to marry? Should Catholic women be allowed their own choice regarding birth control?

Again, we suggest that you write down whatever has irritated you the most about your own religion or others. Then candidly consider your own levels of tolerance, bigotry, and spiritual pride. A look into history may aid in such introspection.

ETHICS AND MORALITY

There is no clear-cut differentiation between morality and ethics. In many instances the words are used interchangeably. However, we would prefer to use the term "ethics" here in regard to codes of conduct or behavior as in "medical ethics," "business ethics," etc. Morality will be considered in relation to all forms of vice, such as gambling, theft, trafficking in drugs, trafficking in illegal or stolen merchandise, loan-sharking, extortion, blackmail—illegal activities in general, like bootlegging, confidence games, etc.

Do you have one set of business ethics for yourself and your own racial or ethnic group and another set for others? (Consider the tribal aspects portrayed in *The Godfather*.)

Do you say to your children, "Do as I say—not as I do?"

Have you ever—

Cheated on an examination?
Fudged on your income tax?

Lied about your age?
Lied about your marital status?
Committed an illegal act?
Ignored a traffic ticket?
Engaged in fraud or forgery or embezzled funds?
Padded an expense account?
Worn falsies?
Ignored a store clerk's error in your favor?
Impersonated another individual?
Spied or eavesdropped on anyone?
Opened another person's mail with malicious intentions?
Intentionally injured or killed someone?
Committed an act of vandalism?
Intentionally injured or killed an animal?
Bullied or abused someone?
Gotten someone fired or demoted because you didn't like them?
Taken a kickback?
Spread malicious gossip or given false testimony?
Intentionally slandered another person or group?
Engaged in harassment, coercion, or mental torture of another?
Enjoyed seeing someone suffer misfortune or disgrace?
Refused to aid someone in distress?
Wished a relative were dead so you would have their money or possessions?
Cheated while playing cards? Golf?
Misrepresented yourself to a prospective employer?
Knowingly "used" someone or taken advantage of them?
(Add any others you might think of.)

Finally, what is the meanest, most unethical, vengeful, or immoral act you've ever committed? And, conversely, what is the most loving act you've ever done?

Someone once stated that the true test of a man's character was what he would do if he knew *for certain* that he would never be found out. Think about it! The first time I saw that I said to myself, "I am a rascal!" Now, years later, I see the wisdom involved. For in the final analysis our character can only be built or torn down, tested or rejected, accepted or condemned—by self. We are, individually, both our own worst enemy and sternest, yet fairest judge. Again the concept of the "two-edged sword" in action applies. For if we truly come to know self we will know which edge of the sword we are riding on—and why—and whether we are moving with God or not.

Finally, there is that beautiful statement in the readings that, "If God is with you then you are already in the majority."

Chapter IV

Understanding Past Life Experience

As love is the expression for experience in life manifested in the earth, so is the experience of the soul in the earth dependent upon that plane, that experience (in earth) as to its race or color or sex. For if there has been the error in that phase, in that expression, the error must be met. For indeed as has been given, *whatsoever ye sow, so shall ye reap.* (294–189)

Many of the individuals who were given readings were said to have been in the earth before—even with the Master during various of His incarnations. For them it was stated:

The promise is, as was given of Him—"For I will bring to remembrance all things whatsoever has been my part with you, for in such manifestations is my Father glorified in you.

And in the same reading,

As was given by Him, let thine works, thine efforts, be even as was said by Him, "If ye will not believe me, ye will believe for the very works' sake—for the things I do bespeak that I believe I AM!" (262–12)

The following was given January 7, 1944, for a woman born June 19, 1915.

What an unusual record—For the entity was one of the eight souls in the Ark!

For as has been given from the beginning, the deluge was not a myth (as many would have you believe) but a period (in Atlantis) when man had belittled himself with the cares of the world, with the deceitfulness of his own knowledge and power, as to require that there be a return to his dependence wholly—physically and mentally—upon the Creative Forces.

Will this entity see such again occur in the earth? Will it be among those who may be given those directions as to how, where, the *elect* may be preserved for the replenishing again of the earth? REMEMBER, NOT *BY WATER*—for it is the mother of life in the earth BUT RATHER BY THE ELEMENT, *FIRE*. (3653–1)

According to the Cayce materials, Atlantis broke up and sank after three major upheavals, the second of which occurred 26,000 years ago, the third and last just about halfway between then and now. The second breakup was recorded in Genesis as the Flood. (The 26,-000 is interesting in that it represents a full Zodiacal cycle of the equinoxes.)

Q: Why in early childhood did I dream so many times that the world was being destroyed, always seeing a black destructive cloud?
A: From the experience in the Atlantean land, when there were those destructive forces as indicated. The entity saw or lived through those experiences of at least two, yea three of the destructive periods; saw the land breaking up, as it were. (823–1)

(In Atlantis) the entity lost, for it longed for and determined within itself it would never again in material experiences love those that could disappoint and bring experiences that would cause the heartache in the flesh. (1747–3)

Before that the entity was in the English land during the period of the First Crusade. . . .

From that sojurn the entity will find itself at times becoming *overzealous* of something that may deal with religion. . . .

Well if such had learned that the lesson given of old by GAMALIEL—*"IF IT BE OF GOD IT WILL CARRY ON, IF IT BE OF MAN IT WILL OF ITSELF FAIL. AND, IF OF GOD WE WOULD ONLY BE FIGHTING AGAINST GOD!" The influences and powers then in the earth indicate purposes, purposes! O WHAT CRIMES HAVE BEEN COMMITTED IN THE NAME OF RELIGION!* (3344–1)

In England, during Crusades, the entity learned much, *that they who fight, they who war against their brethren find themselves warring as against the spirit of truth.* For that as is sown in dread, must be reaped in turmoil and in strife. (1226–1)

Q: To what extent am I permanently influenced by former unhappy experiences?
A: As these are allowed to become a part of the warp and woof of the thinking. *Remember, the mind is the builder. They take hold but if these are lost in Him and His promises, not only the physical disturbance of the neurosis may be eliminated, but the influences of unhappy experiences may become as nothing.* (2269–1)

Or, as the Chinese saying goes, "It doesn't matter—because it doesn't matter."

As to the experiences in the earth, these have been many and quite varied. Many of these are not well even to be known to self, and thus have they been blotted from the book of thy remembrance—*even as He blots them from the book of God's remembrance—if ye love one another,* if ye mete to thy fellowman, yea, to thy sisters in all walks of experience, that love of which ye are capable in thine self. For he who hath loved much, to that one may much be given. (5231–1)

For the entity before this was a patron saint of France, and yet so lazy as to (have this laziness still) be expressed in the present. (3202–1)

Q: What is the purpose of this incarnation?
A: (As) you have been given: The meeting of self and to blot out resentments.
Q: What particular lesson am I to learn from this condition?
A: Tolerance and love. (2872–3)

As a small child I had a great love of ships and bodies of water. To be sure my father was a sailor on the Great Lakes, an engineer, but my fascination was with sailing ships of all kinds, but not the modern steam-driven ones. No one ever taught me to handle a sailboat; I just knew. No one taught me to swim. At age six, alone, I went to the drop-off end of a sandbar, picked up my feet and swam. Foolhardy perhaps, but I've a healthy respect for currents, tides, and the power of the sea. Over the years I've had dreams of being on an ancient ship, single masted, with a tiller rather than a wheel for steering— the likes of which I've never seen in this lifetime. Only a dream, a symbol? Possibly, but I feel very strongly that I've spent past lives on ships such as these and traversed many of the seas of our planet. This has been told me, too, by psychics who knew nothing of my feelings regarding the sea. And in actuality, to date I've never taken an ocean trip—nothing larger than the Great Lakes. Yet, here is the sort of example which can best be used in coming to an awareness and understanding of where we have been before.

One of the most fascinating detective mystery stories you could possibly write is the search within your own self, for where and who you might have been in the past. If you don't want to know, that's all right. You may have good reasons for preferring not to be reminded of it. But if you choose to pursue such adventure you may even come up with a known historical personage—and there have been enough of them down through history to give practically everyone who seeks, a chance for at least one of them, which is all right too, even if you are wrong.

You might go to a psychic who could be just as wrong about your Akashic record as you are. So we suggest you do it yourself. It can be much better for your personal soul development *and* it won't cost you money.

But there are pitfalls. The problem of searching into self for past personalities is balanced on one side by the need to know—for a better understanding of self—and on the other by a kind of curiosity which can take the form of an ego trip. There can be danger, too, in going to a psychic reader who reads you only too well and reveals details that are best left forgotten. Psychedelic drugs can seemingly do the same thing. The present personality may not be able to handle such memories, and I submit to you that mental illness—the number one disease in our nation today*—is not mainly the result of the individual's inability to cope with our complex society. Rather it is the refusal of the conscious/subconscious entity to resolve past life experiences with its present spiritual purposes for incarnating, along with an overall quickening of humanity's unconscious psychic levels of activity at this time in history.

Our suggestion here (and this is the author's opinion, as there is no Edgar Cayce to do it for us) is that those of us who care to make an attempt at seeking past personalities and experiences, accept a mild ego trip for the sake of making a point of reference to our most negative, destructive attitudes and emotions (also our positive talents and attributes). The important thing is to identify an historical character, known or unknown, with your own present life and personality, using yourself as the logical

* At any given time in this country there are more hospital beds occupied by mental patients than for all the rest of the diseases combined. "While only about 2 percent of all hospital admissions are for psychiatric disorders, about one half of the hospital beds in the country are occupied by mentally ill patients. In addition 1-1/2 million adults and children visit outpatient clinics and private physicians for psychiatric diagnosis and treatment each year."—John Hanlon, *Principles of Public Health Administration* (St. Louis, C. V. Mosby Company, 1964) p. 626.

Karmic result of that individual's return. (You might even warm up to it with a parlor game using well-known celebrities—and trying to guess who they might have been.)

We have a close friend who identifies quite strongly with Henry VIII and we engage in some good-natured ribbing about the eventuality of some of Henry's well-publicized foibles catching up with him. Our present friend hasn't had six wives—only one, who loves him dearly. Yet for years his insecurity, jealousy and suspicions regarding her caused both him and his wife no end of torment. We could identify her also with someone who merited such accusations from behavior in past lifetimes. In other words, it's not necessary even to put a known name on the character you were—just make up your own figure whose past life might account for your being as you are or have been in this lifetime.

From the standpoint of the Cayce materials we would recommend two initial books for study along this line of reasoning: *Many Mansions* by Gina Cerminara and *Edgar Cayce's Story of Karma* by Mary Ann Woodward. Most of the following Karmic summaries are drawn from this material. These are representative of present problems and only a few were named as actual historical figures.

CONDITION	KARMIC HISTORY
Racial bigot	As a galley slave beaten to death by a Negro overseer
Homosexual	Mocked such individuals as a satrist and cartoonist in France
Blindness	Had blinded captives with red hot irons
Paralysis	Injured others so they could barely walk
Digestive weakness	Lives of gluttony
Anemia	Shed others' blood

Deafness	Closed ears to others' pleas for aid
Asthma	Pressed the life out of others
Choking spasms	Strangled others to death
Fear of darkness	Confined to dungeons
Fear of water	Died drowning
Claustrophobia	Buried alive
Fear of knives	Killed by sword
Sexually frigid	Forced to wear a chastity belt
Fear of large animals	Died in Roman arena
Fear of Negroes	African, sold other tribes into slavery
Fear of snakes	Died of cobra bite
Mongoloid child	"An entity meeting its own self"
Chronic bed-wetting	Had ducked witches in New England
Anti-Semitic	Had been a Samaritan
Woman, wary of men	Deserted by husband in Crusade period
Distrustful of others	Persecuted, mistreated by others
Uncommunicative	Maintained silence as a Quaker
Much personal charm	Court jester to Henry VIII
Inferiority feelings	So treated by others and accepted it
Aloneness, cut off	Committed suicide
Repeated disappointments	Disappointed others
Life of degradation	Virtuous, but condemned others for licentiousness
Nervous breakdown	Intolerant of others' weaknesses
Epilepsy	Sexual excesses
Epilepsy	Misuse of psychic powers
Mental illness	Practiced witchcraft (Black Magic)

Poverty	Abused authority, impoverished others
Paraplegic	Roman soldier, made light of others' suffering
Cancer	Laughed at Christians being torn by wild animals
Preoccupation with flying (female)	Had been a pilot in Atlantis
Mulatto, crippled	White slave holder, mistreated slaves
Roman. Persecuted early Christians	Roman. Sent others to the arena
Young man, totally paralyzed at age twenty-four in auto accident, spent last eighteen years of his life treated by Christian charities.	Autistic child, bedridden from birth, lived to adulthood, cared for by nurse whose reading said she had been sacrificed in Roman arena.

With this basic background we're ready to begin laying the groundwork for our own personal book of Karma. Thinking back to childhood, and on into adulthood, write down the most outstanding or memorable things you can recall.

1. What things fascinated or interested you most? (I've mentioned water and ships in my case.)

2. What experience or experiences stand out in memory that startled or affected you—and you don't know why?

3. What talents or natural abilities were shown at an early age?

4. Impressive or recurring dreams. Visions—recall of past lives? (My sailing-ship dream, for example.)

5. Strong likes or dislikes?

6. Inventiveness or industriousness?

7. Favorite haunts? Favorite pets or animals?

8. Occupational desires? Chore you most hated.

9. Worst enemy? Best friend?

10. Greatest accomplishment? Biggest disappointment?

11. Greatest fears?

12. Destructive tendencies?

The following are areas for specific consideration as to strong likes and dislikes. They offer clues to our past if we ask ourselves, "If I were totally free to do as I pleased for only twenty-four hours, and had all the money I needed, where would I go (even in time), what would I do, what would I surround myself with, and what would I aspire to be?" (Historical novels and period motion pictures can offer some excellent clues here.)

At the same time, what would I avoid or be repulsed by?

1. Nations, geographical surrounds (mountains, woods, plains, etc.)?

2. Historical periods?

3. Races, religions, nationalities?

4. Occupations, professions?

5. Natural surroundings? Animals?

6. Food and drink? Tastes and smells?

7. Furniture, clothing, material possessions—jewelry, guns, knives, etc.?

8. Music, sounds, singing, playing, listening?

9. Architecture, mathematics?

10. Academic subjects? Artistic forms?

11. Sports, hobbies, friendships?

12. Travel, exploration, study?

13. Creativity, forms of expression and communication?

Finally, if you had seven lifetimes to live in the past, where would you like to have been? Try listing them.

ASTROLOGICAL CONSIDERATIONS

It would be well, also, to study your astrological makeup in order to better understand what planets or signs of the zodiac may be influential in your life at present. This is not easily or simply accomplished, the study of astrology being a major task in itself. However, the following readings will give some insight into the importance astrology was given in the Cayce materials. Note here also that the readings indicated that at least thirty incarnations were necessary for our attaining the full experience in the earth plane! (Reference to readings #2982 and 1861–12)

Consider this reading as it relates to the mental attributes associated with the sensory system as opposed to the emotional, or earth body:

The appearances, or sojourns in the earth, are expressed or manifested through the senses, in the material body.

Do understand and *do interpret the differences between the emotions that arise from the sensory system and those that arise from the glandular system alone.*

True, *physically these interchange. Yet one* (the glandular or emotional) *represents the whole of the development, and the other* (sensory or mental) *represents the step-by-step activity of an entity in its activities through the material world.*

The awarenesses are a pattern of what we call astrological aspects. *Not because an entity, in physical consciousness, sojourned in any of the planets which are a part of this present solar experience.* But each planet is credited with certain environmental influences represented in the characteristics of each individual entity or soul.

Thus, just as we find in this entity: they (the planetary vibrations) give expression through abilities manifested in the material body, in respect to developments or attunements in the glandular system of the body, for material expression.

Thus upon the skein of time and space, the record of each soul is made. In patience and persistence such a record may be read. (2620–2)

The indication given here is that the consciousness developed between earthly lives is a step-by-step progression, within an individual, of a very personal nature (each entity's reactions being different to an equal set of circumstances). Therefore, no two souls would react the same in the earth having both returned from an interplanetary experience represented by, say, Venus or Mars.

Additionally, this step-by-step sensory awareness is combined in the earth with all the past earthly life experiences which are programmed in memory within the glandular (emotional) cells of the body. Consequently, any attempt to resolve astrological aspects without a full knowledge of the past lives and reactions to them can be rather misleading, according to the readings.

In giving that which may be helpful to this entity in the present experience, respecting the sojourns in the earth, it is well that the planetary or astrological aspects also be given. *It should be understood, then, that the sojourning of the soul in that (planetary environ), rather than the position (square, trine or planets at birth, etc.) makes for a greater influence in the experience of an entity or body, in any given plane.*

This is not to belittle that which has been the study of the ancients, but rather it is to give the understanding of same. And, as we have indicated: it is not so much (important) that an entity is influenced because the Moon is in Aquarius or the Sun in Capricorn; or Venus or Mercury in that or the other house or sign; or the Moon in Sun sign; or that one of the planets is in this or that position in the heavens. But rather because those positions in the heavens are from the entity having been in that consciousness in the sojourn as a soul!

This is how the planets have the greater influence in the earth upon the entity, see? *For the application of an experience is what makes for development of a body, a mind, or a soul.* (630)

It should be understood that the earthly-sojourn urges are (pertain) to the emotions; while the mental or innate urges are from the soul's experiences in the environs about the earth. But these are merely urges or inclinations and not impelling forces. Used in their proper relationships as warnings or as things to embrace, they may be applied in the experience as helpful forces and influences.

Know, however, that . . . what the will does about what is set as its ideal—in mental and material as well as spiritual experiences—and then having the courage to carry out that ideal: this makes the difference, between constructive and creative relationships, and those that make one rather a drifter, or ne'er-do-well, or one very unstable and unhappy. (1401–1)

And again, the will as applied to the Ideal.

> The influence from any (planet) is from whatever one from which the soul-and-spirit return, to bring the individual force to the earth. As the spirit is breathed into the body, whence did it come? That is the influence; not the revolution-ideas given by those who study those planetary forces. (3744)

The more important planetary influences in one's horoscope (Author's interpretation) were listed as: 1. Those in the sun signs; 2. Those ascending, or in the rising sign (first house); and 3. Those at the zenith, or top, of the natal chart.

> The strongest of such powers in the destiny of man is: first, the Sun. Then the planets closer, or those that are coming to ascendancy at the time of birth. (254-2)

> *But let it be understood here: no action of any planet or phase of the Sun, Moon or heavenly body surpasses the rulership of man's individual willpower.* For this is the power given by the Creator to man, in the beginning when he became a living soul, with the power to choose for himself.

> The inclinations of man, then, are ruled by the planets under which he was born. To this extent, the destiny of man lies within the scope or sphere of the planets. Given a position of the solar system at the time of the individual's birth, it can be worked out—that is, the inclinations and actions (can be worked out), without regard to the power of the will, or without the will being taken into consideration. (3744)

INFLUENCE OF CUSPS

> This entity comes upon the cusps; thus we find at times conflicting emotions with the entity. During the formative period of mental and physical development, we find that the entity may be easily led. (2411-1)

From the astrological aspects, we find the entity almost exactly upon the cusps. Hence we will find two influences, and the entity oft needing or requiring consideration by those making the choice of environs for the entity during the early portion of its development. . . . For there has been given into the keeping an entity who may mean as much to the world as the entity meant to—means to—America. (1208–1)

AWARENESS OR CONSCIOUSNESS BETWEEN INCARNATIONS

Then there are the sojourns in the other realms of the solar system which represent certain attributes. *Not that ye maintain a physical earth-body in Mercury, Venus, Jupiter, Uranus, or Saturn. There is, however, an awareness or consciousness in those realms, when absent from the body;* and there is a response to the position those planets occupy in this solar system.

Hence ye often find in thy experiences that places, peoples, things and conditions seem a part of self, as if ye had been in the consciousness of them. (2823–1)

Just as an entity's attendance at this or that university . . . would make for a parlance peculiar to itself, even though individuals might study the same line of thought—but one attending Harvard, another Yale, another Oxford, another Stanford, another the University of Arizona. They each would carry with them the vibrations created by their activity in those environments. In the same way, *emotions arise from . . . activity in a particular sojourn; and are called the spirit of the institution to which the entity has betaken itself.* . . . So we find those astrological sojourns making for those vibrations or impressions in the present entity. (633–2)

Each entity is a part of the Universal Whole. Then all the knowledge and understanding which has ever been a part of the entity's consciousness has a part in the entity's experience. *Thus unfoldment, in the present, consists merely in becoming aware of experiences through which the entity has passed, in any consciousness, either in body or in mind.* (2823-1)

Appearances in the earth few and far between. This accounts for the sereneness of the entity even under great stress. (3245-1)

WILLPOWER

The inclinations of man are ruled by the planets under which he is born, for the destiny of man lies within the sphere or scope of the planets . . . *but let there be understood here—no action of any planet, or the phases of the sun, the moon, or any of the heavenly bodies, surpasses the rule of man's willpower.* (3744-3)

As has been indicated by some, ye are part and parcel of a Universal Consciousness, or God. And thus (part) of all that is within the Universal Consciousness, or Universal Awareness: as are the stars, the planets, the sun and the moon.

Do ye rule them or do they rule thee? They were made for thine own use, as an individual. Yea, that is the part (they play), the thought which thy Maker, thy Father-God thinks of thee. *For ye are as a corpuscle in the body of God; thus a co-creator with Him, in what ye think and in what ye do.* (2794-3)

FREE WILL AND STAGES OF DEVELOPMENT

Astronomy is considered a science, and astrology foolishness. Which is correct? One (the science) holds that because of the position of the earth, the sun, and the planets, they are balanced one with another in some manner or some way—yet that they have nothing to do with man's life, or the expanse of life, or the emotions of the physical being in the earth.

Then why and how do the effects of the sun so greatly influence other life in the earth—and not affect man's life and man's emotions?

Since the sun has been set as the ruler of this solar system, *does it not appear reasonable that it does have an effect upon the inhabitants of the earth,* as well as upon plant and mineral life in the earth? . . . Thus we find given in the Bible: *"the sun and the moon and the stars were made also";* this being the writers attempt to convey to the individual the realization that there is also an influence in their activity.

For remember: they . . . the sun, the moon, and the planets . . . have their marching orders from the Divine, and they move in these. Man alone is given the birthright of free will. He, alone, may defy his God. (5757-1)

The shadows of those things, from the sojourns of this entity in Mercury, Jupiter, Saturn, Venus, and the moon, have their portion (influence) in the relationship and activity of the entity. These (astrological influences) are only the mental urges that arise, and become the individuality of an entity as it expresses in the material world. (On the other hand), the appearances in the earth, through various sojourns, that have become active in the experience . . . at any one given place, position, appearance, or period, are but as the personality in the entity's experience . . . and are as urges from emotions that have been created. (633–2)

Being absent from the material body is manifested in what we call astrological aspects, which become a phase of each and every soul and are signposts along the individual way. For . . . all of these are a part of thy heritage, thy innate urges—that arise from and produce influences in the material experience in the present. (1745–1)

For without passing through each and every (astrological) stage of development, there is not the correct vi-

bration to become one with the Father. . . . Then in the many stages of development throughout the Universe or in the great system of the Universal Forces, each stage of development is made manifest through flesh—which is the testing portion of the Universal Vibration. In this manner, then, and for this reason, all are made manifest in flesh and there is the development through aeons of time and space, called Eternity. (3744)

For it is not strange that music, color, and vibration are a part—and a pattern—of the whole universe.

Hence the entity passes through those stages which some have seen as planes, some as steps, some have seen as cycles, and others have experienced as places. (5755-1)

THE PLANETS

MERCURY

Mercury brings the high mental abilities; the faculties that at times may become a development for the soul, or at other times be turned towards aggrandizement of selfish interests. For the entity is among those who have entered during those years when there was the great entrance of those who have risen high in their abilities (Atlanteans), and who are then passing through the periods when there must be application of the will, else the very abilities that have been maintained in the sun and Mercurian influences will become as stumbling blocks. (633-2)

In Jupiter, we find the great ennobling conditions; those which would bring money and the influence for good into the life. We find in Neptune the mysticism, mystery, spiritual insight, and spiritual development.

The Mercury influence giving the mental understanding of each.

Then, with a mental insight into the operative elements of ennoblement—the virtues, the good and the beautiful; along with the mysteries of the universal energies; and with the understanding of these; there is brought development to the soul. For the soul feeds upon that environment to which the mind guides and directs. (900–14)

VENUS

In the astrological aspects, we find that through influences from sojourns in the Venus environs, the entity is a lover of beauty, especially of song . . . should be given training . . . for the awakening of the entity in those influences, for the use of the entity's voice in praise and in thanksgiving. Hence all things that have to do with man's ability to express in beautiful ways and manners will be of interest . . . whether pertaining to nature, voice, or song—or even to art subjects. (1990–3)

In Venus the body-form is near to that (which is) in the three-dimensional plane. For it is what may be said to be rather all-inclusive! For it is what ye would call love, which, to be sure, may be licentious and selfish; but which also may be so large and so inclusive as to take on less of self and more of the ideal-more of that which is giving.

What is love? Then what is Venus? It is beauty, love, hope, charity—yet all of these have their extremes. But these extremes are not in the nature or manner . . . found in the tone or attunement of Uranus (the planet of extremes); for these, in Venus, are more in an order so that they blend one with another. (5755–1)

MARS

Astrologically we find Mars, Mercury, Venus, and Jupiter—and note their importance. (Their order—the entity entered from Mars.) Anger may upset the body and cause a great deal of disturbance, to others as well as self. *Be angry, but sin not.* You will learn it only in patience and self-possession. (3621–1)

JUPITER

In Jupiter, we find the great ennobling influences— the broadmindedness, the ability to consider others, the Universal Consciousnesses that are a part of the entity's unfoldment. (1890–2)

In Jupiter we find the associations making for tendencies towards large groups . . . in relationship with the entity. This also makes for inclinations that there will be great amounts of this world's good in the entity's experiences. . . . The training also should be, then, not only in the teen ages but throughout its development . . . as to the use of same (wealth)—as its being lent from Creative Forces and energies, and not for self-indulgence. (1206–3)

SATURN

In Saturn we find the sudden or violent changes— those influences and environs that do not grow, as it were, but are sudden by change of circumstances materially—or by activities apparently on the part of others, that become a part of self by the very associations. Yet these are testing periods of thy endurance, or thy patience, or thy love of truth, harmony, and the spirit that faileth not. From the combination of this with Uranus, we find the extremes; the material or mental environs in which the very opposites may be expected. *Remember, only in Christ Jesus do extremes meet.* (1981–1)

URANUS

(Combined Influences)

In the astrological activities that produce . . . these experiences (desire for travel, desire for change) as innate, we find Uranus, Neptune, and Saturn as ruling influences; which make for interest in—yet fear of—occult and mystic forces. But rather (let it be) the expression of the psychic than the occult or mystic . . . for . . . the greater development. . . . For in Uranus we find the extremes—and when the entity is very good, it's very, very good.

Then those things of the experience must be tempered by . . . the Venus influence. Although these are latent, they should find the greater expression; also the urges from Saturn would make for the entity having many homes, or many marriages . . . for consistency and persistency are the sisters of patience, and patience the entity needs to learn as its lesson in this experience. (1431–1)

From Uranian influences we find the extremist. And these tendencies . . . will develop especially through the early teen-age years, when there will be moods . . . and wonderments. . . . These Uranian (tendencies) also make for intuitive influences and the ability to develop the psychic forces of the entity. (1206–3)

Those who have exceptional abilities with Uranian influence may be said also to . . . have exceptional abilities to err, or to be led astray, in the direction not best for . . . self's development. (38–1)

In Uranus we find the extremes and the interest in the occult, the mystical. This is well if it is balanced in the spiritual nature. (2571–1)

As to astrological, then: we find the entity comes under the influence of Mercury, Jupiter, Saturn, Venus, and Uranus. . . . In the Uranian influences, periods are wrought when there seems to be every condition imaginable awry—whether business relations, social ones, or financial. Everything seems awry! Again, there are seasons when most things come too easy. (5–2)

In Uranus we find the extremes. Thus the entity in spiritual, mental, and in material things, finds periods when it is on the mountain tops—and again in the depths of despair. (3706-2)

Uranus is said to be the ruler of Aquarius, consequently becoming more influential as the Aquarian age emerges.

NEPTUNE

The soul and spirit took its flight from faraway exercised forces in Neptune. Hence we have an entity that will seem peculiar to other people, and will rarely ever be understood. Yet she has the spiritual insight for developing in the earth plane, and she is one by whom many could be benefited from being in contact with her. (2553-1)

In Neptune we find the inclination towards things that have to do with water, and over water, and to be on waters. . . . These, then, give an urge—again as through Saturn—for change of scene and change of environment—and the desire for travel . . . the things that are exciting, that pertain to the heroic and hero worship. This urge must ever be tempered by directing the entity to the character of ideals. (1426-1)

PLUTO

Q: Just what are the effects of Pluto, in conjunction with one's ascendant?
A: This, as we find, is entirely amiss (different) from what we might call a physical expression; but, as we find indicated, these (influences) are a development that is occurring in the universe, or environs about the earth—Pluto. Not, as some have indicated, that it is gradually being dissipated. It is gradually growing, and thus is one of those influences that are to be a demonstrative activity in the future affairs or developments of man, towards the spiritual-minded influence, or those influences outside of himself.

These (individuals) in the present, as might be said, are merely the (ones) becoming aware of same. Rather, within the next hundred to two hundred years there may be a great deal of influence (of Pluto) upon the ascendancy of man; for it's closest of those to the activities of the earth, to be sure, and is a developing influence, not one already established. (1100–27)

SPIRITUAL DEVELOPMENT

(Planetary Aspects)

In the development, then, that man may be one with the Father, (it is) necessary that the soul pass—with its companion, the will—through all the various stages of development, until the will is lost in Him, and he becomes one with the Father.

The illustration of this we find in the man called Jesus. This man, as man, makes the will the will of the Father; then becoming one with the Father, and the model for man. . . .

When the soul (of the Master) reached that development which it reached in earth's plane, it became the model in the flesh, as it had reached through developments in those spheres, or planets known in the earth's plane, obtaining then the One in All.

As in Mercury pertaining of mind
In Mars of madness
In Earth as of flesh
In Venus as love
In Jupiter as strength
In Saturn as the beginning of earthly woes, that to which all insufficient matter is cast for the beginning.
In that of Uranus as of the psychic
In that of Neptune as of mystic
In Septimus (Pluto) as of consciousness
In Arcturus as of the developing. (900–10)

CHRIST-CONSCIOUSNESS

Q: The problem which concerns the proper symbols, or similies, for the Master, the Christ. Should Jesus be described as the Soul who first went through the cycle of earthly lives to attain perfection including perfection in the planetary lives also?
A: He should be. This is as the man (he was), see?
Q: Should this be described as a voluntary mission (on the part of) One Who was already perfected and returned to God, having accomplished His oneness in other planes and systems?
A: Correct.
Q: Should the Christ-consciousness be described as the awareness within each soul, imprinted in pattern on the mind and waiting to be awakened by the will, of the soul's oneness with God?
A: Correct. That's the idea exactly. (5749–14)

ONENESS OF ALL FORCE

Q: What are the laws governing relativity of all force?
A: In giving the manifestation of such a law, which does exist, we first must consider that (which) is called force, and that force then in its relation, or the relativity of that force to all force.

There were set in the beginning, as far as the concern is of this physical earth plane, those rules or laws in the relative force of those that govern the earth, and the beings of the earth plane, and also that same law governs the planets, stars, constellations, groups, and those that constitute the sphere, the space, in which the planets move. These are of one force, and we see the manifestation of the relation of one force with another in the many various phases as is shown (here in the readings), *for in fact that which to the human mind exists, in fact does not exist, for it has been in past before it is to the human mind in existence.*

In this we see the law of the relations of conditions, space or time and its relation to human mind, as is capable of obtaining information upon the earth plane from a normal force or condition. Hence, we bring the same word, relativity of force, to prove its own self, and condition, for we have as in this:

The earth in its motion is held in space by that force of attraction, or detraction, or gravitation, or lack of gravitation in its force, so those things that do appear to have reality, and their reality to the human mind, have in reality passed into past conditions before they have reached the mind, for with the earth's laws, and its relations to other spheres, has to man become a past condition. So it is reached only in the further forces as will shows, and as is given, for man to understand in this developing, or this evolution from sphere to sphere, or from plane to plane, in this condition.

Hence, we find to the normal mind, there is no law as to relativity of force, save as the individual may apply same in the individual's needs of them. That is sufficient.

The study from the human standpoint, of subconscious, subliminal, psychic soul forces, is, and should be the great study for the human family. . . . For *through self man will understand its Maker, when it understands its relation to its Maker. And it will only understand that through itself.* And that understanding is the knowledge as is given here in this state. (3744-4)

SPIRITUAL DEVELOPMENT

(*Psychic Centers*)

Spiritual contact is (made) through the glandular forces of Creative Energies. . . . Thus we find a connection and an association of the spiritual being with the mental self in any of those centers (glandular) from which reflexes react with all of the organs, all of the emotions, all of the activities of a physical body. (263–13)

Each of the seven glands, or psychic centers (chakras), is said to be attuned or related to a planet, as follows:

Jupiter	Pituitary
Mercury	Pineal
Uranus	Thyroid
Venus	Thymus
Mars	Adrenals
Neptune	Leydig
Saturn	Gonads (281)

In this last relationship we complete the circle, in a sense, regarding astrology and its effect upon attitudes and emotions. As the readings indicate, our physical bodies will inform us in no small degree as to the planets that we vibrate to or are attuned to—positively and/or negatively.

Therefore, if our reader desires to pursue the creating of past life associations and identifying with real or imagined personalities, he will have plenty to work with—thirty lifetimes—all the planets and signs of the zodiac, all the inclinations we've listed, and more.

At the same time the readings also indicated (in 1937) that only some 30% of the people in the earth (at that time) would relate to their planetary aspects in classical astrological terms, while some individuals might react in diametrical opposition to their aspects and still others not at all!

Our main point in this exercise of association is this—*and we cannot emphasize the following too strongly*—that after you have accepted any past life or astrological association, real or imagined, then accept it fully (as reality in thought if nothing else—for "thoughts are things" and do exist). And finally—*(Most Important)*—detach yourself from it! Freely, unemotionally, without tears, sentiment or regret, recognizing that what was lived in the past (good, bad, or indifferent as it relates to now) was all part of an experience to be used for soul growth—nothing more, nothing less.

Henry VIII, for example, is gone. The memory of what he experienced in that lifetime still exists, both in the minds of those associated with him, for good or ill, and in his own present consciousness, too. But the soul that was Henry lived other lives, and still has more to go, so that if in the present you care to say, "Yes, I once was Henry, I truly could have been he." O.K., but then say to yourself, "Rest well, friend Henry"—and bid that aspect of self the peace of being allowed to rest, without allowing it to affect your present digestive tract or relationships with your spouse, etc. The same holds true for all our past identifications. And while our suggestions in this chapter, we feel, are extremely valid and important, in no way do we suggest they are easily accomplished or effected without a struggle. (It may take more than just this lifetime!) We suggest you keep laughing through the tears.

As an aid, the readings often pointed to the thirtieth chapter of Deuteronomy and the fourteenth through the seventeenth chapters of John:

For, as the saw goes: Don't tell us what you used to be when things went all your way, but what are you doing today that the Savior may stay with thee and with thy concept of the application of His tenets in the lives of those with whom ye come in contact day by day! For, as ye do it, as ye treat, as ye think of each individual with whom ye come in contact along life's way, that entity—be it one physically attractive or one that casts off influences that are repulsive—is an OPPORTUNITY for YOU, as an individual, to glorify God, and to be aware of the Chris-consciousness enabling you to meet every problem.

As He gave, fears and doubts and disappointments are a part of the price one pays for the opportunity to see life

—or the experience of that man terms life—manifested in individual lives in a material plane. (2082–10)

If we can only come to understand ourselves and others in relation to past experiences (as the Master understood those He came in contact with) then we will have come a long way toward laying the foundation for individual soul growth.

Chapter V

Interpersonal Relationships

If ye would have friends, be friendly! If ye would have others be kind to thee, be kind to them! If ye would know thy Maker, then in gentleness of heart and in sureness of purpose live each day that ye may look to Him and say, "Thy will, O God, be done in me; *not* my will, but *Thy* will." (792–1)

Then let the mental attitude be kept in that way of expecting, in the ability to help others. Happiness is a state of mind attained by giving same to others. (7272–2)

For thou art in thyself divine! The mere fact or knowledge of thy existence in a material world, prompted by the activities or the movement of the Spirit itself, indicates they own divinity; but to be attained! And this may never be done by holding grudges or disputations with any.

For these only bring hardships, as they did in that experience (of Jesus) to those who (not as He) *attempted to take the directing of activities into their own hands.* (1709–2)

Think not that He in the flesh found not stumbling in the mind and in the experience of each of those He chose, even as His representatives in the earth.

As each of the twelve Apostles represented major centers or regions or realms through which consciousness became aware in the body of the earth itself, so did He find—as in thine own self ye find—those twelve stumbling stones, those twelve things that oft not only disgust but disappoint thee—as to the reaction and way people and things react. These are the price of flesh, of material consciousness, and are only passing. Know deep within self that these, too, must pass away, but the beauty, the love, the hope, the faith remains ever. (2823)

The readings indicate, as here noted, that even the Master had problems of His own in His personal relationships with the Disciples. All of which can serve as a lesson in itself. There is a clue, perhaps, in the apocryphal Book of Barnabas, which states that when the Master chose His disciples He picked from among the most sinful of men He could find in order to demonstrate how His teachings could change the lives of men for the better.

In the same manner it seems to us that the entire body of material given through Edgar Cayce stands as testimony to itself, in that if applied as directed it also changes men's lives for the better. Or, as it was written, "By their fruits ye shall know them."

Was the Master faced with difficult people and situations in His life as merely a test of His own divinity and willpower—and remember He stated we *all* are divine, as in, "Know ye not? Ye are Gods?"—or is there possibly a deeper lesson in Truth concealed here for our awakening?

How often have we observed in our own lives and in the lives of others that the most difficult situations imaginable can result eventually in the greatest personal attainment and in retrospect, the greatest acclaim or personal satisfaction? For Jesus, the most difficult decision was His choice to go into Jerusalem and face crucifixion (as opposed to the wishes of His disciples). His decision and ultimate accomplishment was the Glory of the Resurrection—in becoming the Risen Christ.

What would have happened if He had gone along with Peter's wishes (and the others') and had not returned to

Jerusalem? A missed opportunity—a chance then to save all mankind lost until some later time and place, some other lifetime? It could have happened that way if He had served self and His close advisers rather than following His own inner guidance—the Will of the Father.

It seems to us that in many smaller ways each of us are given similar opportunities, especially with somewhat difficult people and situations. How often have we seen in a business or professional situation that the ideal person from the standpoint of talent, training, capability, and desire was kept from a specific spot or advancement primarily because someone in authority found "something he didn't like" about them? *And* at the same time the individual or establishment who rejected, thwarted, or fired such a person served to lose most in the long run, thus missing an opportunity for mutual advancements. (For example, if the University of Notre Dame insisted that all its staff be Catholics they never would have hired Knute Rockne as their football coach or the current, very successful Ara Parseghian!)

Or, if Jesus had looked at Peter and said to Himself, "No, this is a person who will eventually deny me and run for his life"—then where would we be?

Our point is that Jesus took a risk, indeed a number of risks in various important decisions—in choosing His disciples, in going into Jerusalem, and finally in allowing Himself to be scourged, reviled and slain.

The indication from the standpoint of the Cayce materials is that at the final moment the Master suffered a death that none of us need ever know—because of His purpose in the earth—a complete severance from the Father; spiritual death. Then with His love and dedication and power He picked up what He had to offer (His purified body) and went to preach for three days in the borderlands—Hell, Purgatory—to lost souls everywhere, remembering the promises that, "Yea, though I descend to the very bowels of Hell, Thou shalt be with me." It was only then, after those three days, that He was resurrected by the grace of our Father's love. In the interim he was seen by Mary Magdalene, who was told not to touch him as He "had not yet ascended to the Father," Sunday not being three full days after His death.

And so, Jesus fully understood faith, decision, and what it meant to take a risk—complete faith and acceptance of the Father's will and the guidance thereof. Which leads us to what we feel is a particularly deep insight into interpersonal relationships—first formulated by Mr. Lewis Mortenson of East Petersburg, Pennsylvania, and presented as "A Theory of Interpersonal Dynamics" in ARE lectures by Dr. Lindsay Jacob. We are deeply indebted to both gentlemen for these concepts and their permission to include them here along with our own material:

A. A "risk" decision is the ability to give up one value for another without a residue of regret.

B. A "safety seeking" decision is the result of the inability (or fear) to trade value for value. Sometimes expressed as "Having one's cake and eating it too."

C. The immediate motivation of all human action is a decision. (Indecision, vacillation, or inconsistency tend to create static or chaos in human relations.)

D. A social unit is composed of at least two persons in a functioning relationship—which is governed by several specific and dynamic rules:

1.a. At any given moment, one functioning position is dominant (positive) and directive.

 b. The other functioning position is directed (receptive/negative) and responsive.

2.a. The dominant position is always single in nature.

 b. The responsive (or receptive/negative) position may be single or multiple in nature.

3.a. The dominant position will effect either growth or depletion, depending upon whether the motivating factor was a "risk" decision or a "safety seeking" decision.

 b. The responsive position will result in growth or depletion dependent upon the acceptance or rejection of a "risk" or "safety seeking" decision.

4.a. The cause of an unhealthy relationship is a "safety seeking" decision.

  b. The key to the creation of a healthy relationship—or the dissolution of an unhealthy relationship—is a "risk" decision.

5. Control of the relationship is held by the dominant individual, however the responsive party holds the keystone to the relationship.

A careful analysis of the interaction of any group of people (business, social, personal, political, etc.) will invariably break into a pattern of two-group situations. That is, no matter how complex the situation, it breaks down finally to a set of two parties—one of whom is dominant for the particular moment, and the other responsive or submissive. Another way to express the dominant/responsive relationship would be as power versus love. The dominant party will invariably revolve around a single individual or leader—whereas the responsive party will fragment itself around a number of individuals or responsive actions and opinions.

This holds true especially in person-to-person or partnership relationships. The control of the relationship is held by the dominant individual, but the keystone to that relationship is held by the one who is responding in either a receptive or a negative manner. In other words, the controlling dominant individual cannot effectively convey his direction, information, attitudes, emotions, etc. to the responsive party unless or until the responsive one first agrees to receive it. (As in, "You can lead a mule to water, but you can't make him drink—you can lead a boy to school, but you can't make him think!")

From this we observe that our basic human freedom is the choice of whether or not (and how) to respond to whatever individual dominance or ideas of dominance we may meet as we progress through life. Should an individual or organized group attempt to force acceptance, submission, or blind response from us because of "safety-seeking" or "power" decisions on their part, then they are treating us as something less than human and are creating a situation in which growth cannot occur.

First, let this be a criterion of activity by each: He or she, who would—through force—impel another as to way of thinking, or activity, is a tyrant. (254–51)

Forced dominance or tyranny is invariably the result of a threat to a set of personal values held by the dominating individual, resulting in fear and safety-seeking decisions. Again, power versus love. Only through "risk" decisions, which allow the responsive parties to react by free choice, without threat of control or recrimination, can a dominant individual function creatively.

This is very probably the ultimate test of leadership, in leading through love rather than power. And it follows that the saying "Whom the Gods would destroy, they first make mad with power" is very applicable here in relation to safety seeking on the part of any leader. In Jesus' case, though he had all power in heaven and earth. He demonstrated by risking all that we can truly possess only that which we freely give away, and surrendered His power to the will of the Father. As a result He became possessor of that which He is—the Risen Christ; the pattern and Way-show-er for all of us.

Since all human relationships move within this basic dominant-responsive risk-safety-seeking pattern, the relative positions and motives tend to shift from moment to moment depending upon the trend of conversation or the activity involved. If one attends a movie, play, or concert, the position is responsive. But if the role should be reversed and one is directing a movie, performing in a play or concert, then of course the dominant role is asserted and the audience may respond with applause, a rush for the exits, or even a volley of rotten fruit.

Long-term relationships invariably show a preponderance of responsiveness/dominance in either direction by one or both parties. There is that rare creative situation in friendships, partnerships, or marriage, where both parties are mutually responsive to each other at all levels of their combined experience. This could well serve as a defining line for "true love" or that somewhat cliché-ridden term, "a meaningful relationship." Yet, these are conditions worth striving for. In a marriage, for instance, if the partners respond to one another to make a more creative union, they are trading value for value received and growth occurs. On the other hand, if one or both cannot respond creatively, or if the dominant partner asserts self through ultimatums or personal safety-seeking decisions, then the marriage will suffer. The same holds true for all other relationships as well.

A study and overall awareness of these interpersonal concepts will lead to a more clear-cut understanding of why people do what they do in various situations. At the same time such an awareness and understanding will provide the observer with a greater ability to predict individual responsiveness both by self and others.

Consider the subject of health and healing. In a doctor/patient relationship, for example, a physician cannot ordinarily assist a patient unless the patient responsively initiates the relationship by asking for help. Then too, the doctor cannot help the patient unless he in turn responds to the patient's present condition and point of view. *In other words, both parties need to be mutually responsive for healing to occur.* This holds true especially in cases of psychological or psychiatric counseling and should not be overlooked as an important factor in all other forms of healing and medical practice.

Should a psychiatrist, for instance, attempt to force treatment on an unwilling patient, then a situation exists in which little, if any, growth will occur. Once again the key to the relationship is the individual in the responsive position. Another situation arises in which the person who should be responsive insists upon dominance, as when a patient states belligerently, "I've been to a dozen doctors and they haven't done a thing for me! Now show me what you can do!" Obviously, until some change in attitude occurs, the outcome is readily predictable.

Here we return once more to our basic premise—that

individual attitude is the most important factor in human awareness. Following this we agree with Jacob and Mortenson as to the primary importance of "risk decisions" as the determining factor in all interpersonal relationship. These two points should be written in bold letters in our "Book of Life" and well remembered, for we shall be referring to them over and over again in succeeding chapters.

For as ye know, as ye interpret in thine own experience, as in the life of Him (the Master) who—though without fault—was hated of others. "If the world hate me, and it does, it will hate thee." *But if ye hate the world, if ye dislike those with whom ye are associated, then His death, His love, His promise becomes of none effect in thee!*

For the WORLD hath hated Him without a cause, ye feel within thyself that ye are distrusted, that ye are hated without a cause. But if ye do the same in return, His promise becomes of no effect in thee—ye are of the world and not of Him! (3078-1)

Don't lose patience with thy children, thy friends who become impatient. For He did not lose patience with His disciples. (5089-2)

Do not find fault, for when thou findest fault in thy relationships with others, the greater fault is within thee. (370-3)

But if the heart and mind forgive those who despitefully use thee, those that speak evil in diverse places; those that find fault with others will find fault in themselves; for they are writing their own record—(and) they must meet, every one, that which they have said about another; for so is the image, the soul of the Creator in each body, and when ye speak evil of or unkindly to thy brother, thou hast done it unto thy God. (487-17)

The entity is oft quite lonely, for few individuals fully comprehend the depth of thought that the entity finds in even the conversation with others. For the mind of the entity moves on much faster than even words or activities can give expression to. (5055–1)

Q: How can I overcome the lack of ability to make lasting friendships?
A: It's just as has been indicated. They are not things to be overcome, but are to be lived with—until the purpose and import of self is such that "Not of myself but that the Lord, the God that I would see in even the faults of my fellowmen, becomes glorified in that I may do in any activity of a helpful nature in their relations!" Thus comes peace, harmony. (1238–3)

For it is the spirit, the purpose, the ideal with which ye think, ye speak, ye act, that will determine what the fruit of thy life, of thy thoughts, will be. *If ye sow the spirit,* in the seed of the spirit of patience, *of love,* of long-suffering, brotherly kindness, *the lack of hate*— but love—love is everything—*then ye will find,* as He has given, *He the Master, Jesus,* the Christ-consciousness *will abide with thee. He has attained the Christ-consciousness in giving of Himself. Though able in mental and physical to lay aside the cross, He accepted same, offering self as the sacrifice; that ye might have an advocate in the Father.* Thus ye are saved by Grace. (3459–1)

Chapter VI

Home and Family

But don't marry until you have learned to control yourself. For you would attempt to control the little woman, and you won't do it! For they are not to be controlled; they can be led but not driven, Mr.!
(5249-1)

The readings affirm over and over again that the home is truly a spiritual laboratory—that no greater opportunities exist for soul growth in the earth than those found within the framework of family relationships arising within an established home environment. The relative possibilities implied here are unlimited, of course, but each of us should be able to discern certain patterns as he looks into his own past and present home situations.

Our true spiritual home is an at-onement with Father/Mother God. Our family is all mankind, or at least those who would do His bidding, as the Master gave us to understand. Yet within the earth we have ideas to test, attitudes and emotions to understand and build upon, ideals and purposes to pursue. And so it is within the close confines of home and family we "meet self" continually, on a day-by-day basis—as well as over an entire lifetime—to better work out a greater understanding of the creative process.

It's a shame that Freud and Edgar Cayce never met. For there is no more plausible explanation for many deep-rooted Freudian complexes than those found in analyzing current problems from the standpoint of past life situations. Within the Cayce readings we often find a mother living with a husband and son who competed with each other for her hand and affections in some past existence—and the opposite holds true for many father-mother-daughter triangles. Both Oedipus and Electra complexes become readily understandable if we accept the premise that all parties involved had pursued one another in some past life with a certain amount of cutthroat sexual abandon.

Or, consider the parent and child who constantly antagonize each other, with the parent usually holding the upper hand. The readings gave a good number of instances where the roles had been exactly reversed in the past, with the child now meeting that which he had previously dealt out to the other. Siblings, too, show up in varying relationships. A number of readings showed current brothers and sisters to have been mates in times past, their current affections/antagonisms dependent on how they related to one another before. Some other possibilities are equally fascinating.

One member of a family whose members had a considerable number of life readings was said to have been Oliver Cromwell in seventeenth-century England. His sister, living under the same roof with him, was said to have been the wife of Charles I! (You'll recall that Cromwell had Charles dethroned and beheaded!) Our information is that the pair did *not* get along very well.

Not all relationships need have been difficult or problematical. Obviously many home and family situations are extremely happy, cooperative ventures, resulting from much of the same in the past. Some children may remain extremely close to one or both parents all their lives, while others come into a family for various karmic reasons and detach themselves at an early age with no particular regrets or problems.

Still other possibilities arise where one or more individuals in a relationship have reversed sexual roles somewhere along the line, the indication being that an individual can become too masculine or too feminine over the course of numerous lives in one sexual role and thus choose to incarnate in the opposite sex to achieve a better balance. One of the accompanying problems in sex reversal is that the individuals can become confused in their choice of sexual partners—a root cause for homosexuality that Freud never considered, but Cayce did. Consequently, a very masculine type may choose to incarnate as a female only to find that the deeply ingrained past attitudes and emotions toward having sex with females leads to lesbian preferences. Again, the reverse can be true for male homosexuality. This was not the only basis for these conditions that Cayce gave, but it can explain a great proportion of such cases.

Another explanation for many Freudian sex problems can be taken from this reading:

Q: How did the entity's inferiority complex originate?
A: For the fear or dislike of men. You cannot be one who took the vows and kept them and then lightly turn around and try to gratify the appetites of those who are not easily satisfied. (4082-1)

When we consider the number of souls who have lived past lives as members of religious orders and taken the required vows of celibacy (and poverty), we can readily perceive such possibilities of karmic carry-over. (And not only for those who kept the vows; there were others who did not fare so well!)

Q: How can I overcome the fear that besets me, especially about myself and my wife?
A: Fear is the root of most of the ills of mankind, whether of self, of what others think of self, or what self will appear to others. To overcome fear is to fill the mental, spiritual being, with that which wholly casts out fear; that is, as the love that is manifest in the world through Him who gave Himself (as) the ransom of many. Such love, such faith, such understanding, casts out fear. Be ye not fearful; for that thou sowest, that thou must reap. Be more mindful of that sown. (5449-3)

We would suggest here as we have previously that our readers add these questions to their "Book of Life."

What previous relationships can you sense to a greater or lesser degree among the various members of your own family?

Have you sensed any blood relationship with close friends, associates, neighbors, etc.?

Has your family been a closely knit group or otherwise?

Can you point out, within your family, one or more individuals to whom you seem to be more strongly attached? Any whom you have been extremely antagonized by?

Do you have a physical place, with or without people attached, where you truly feel "at home"? In either case, can you explain to yourself why you feel as you do about it?

On the assumption that you could have been born into any family that you have known personally, list five families that you would have enjoyed being part of. Does one family stand out, preferably, above the others? Why? If your own family would not be a preference at all, then why do you feel you were drawn to them?

(Again most likely you'll find questions of your own to add in these areas.)

The following readings concern various aspects of home and family relationships along with material pertinent to previous chapters. They have been included here in a manner which will allow a broader view of the readings themsleves and the type of dialogue that went on between the sleeping Cayce and those who sought his advice.

HOME AND MARRIAGE—GENERAL

Mrs. C.: You will have before you the enquiring minds, present here, (2390), born near . . . Georgia, August 24, 1910, and (2533) born in . . . Virginia, December 22, 1904, together with the information in their past readings. Considering their desire to build together and better fulfill their purposes for entering this time, you will give such information as will be helpful in attaining to their ideal. You will answer the questions that may be asked.

Mr. C.: Yes, we have the entities here (2390), (2533); and that which has been indicated in the experience of each entity. In giving that as may be helpful or beneficial, there are many conditions that should be taken into consideration; especially that premise from which such information may be attained.

All entities—as these two entities—meet for a purpose. As to whether their ideals are the same, in the meeting, does not depend upon the attraction they may have one for the other; rather upon what they have done about their ideal in their associations one with the other in varied experiences, or in some definite period of activity. Whether these have been for weal or woe does not prevent the attraction.

Thus, whether that attraction is to be for the advancement or the undoing of something in themselves depends, again, upon what is the ideal of each.

As we would give, then—the premise is that ideal to which each should in the present opportunity LOOK, HOPE, BE! (2533-7)

Note the emphasis on ideals and purposes in the previous reading, whereas the following one touches on spiritual patterns being built.

Let each budget the time. Let each give so much to the recreation for the body, for the mind, for the social activities, for the necessary activities for the supplying of the needs in their varied relationships. And be *cooperative* one with another in such things.

The marital relationships, as we have indicated, will become an effectual, helpful experience in the life of the entity; as also in the life of the mate, if the coordinations of their activities in such relationships are made as to be sacred in their notions, their ideas, their activities being not for self-indulgences but as a union of that necessary for the creative forces and influences in the experiences of the life of each, as to bring the crowning influence to the experience of each.

In the establishing of the home, make it as that which may be the pattern of a heavenly home. Not as that set aside for only a place to sleep or to rest, but where not only self but all who enter there may feel, may experience, by the very vibrations that are set up by each in the sacredness of the home, a helpfulness, a *hopefulness* in the air *about* the home. As not only a place of rest, not only a place of recreation for the mind, not only a place as a haven for the bodies and minds of both but for all that may be as visitors or as guests. And remember those injunctions that have been in thine sojourns, and be thou mindful of the entertaining of the guests; for some have entertained angels unawares. *Make thine home, thine abode, where an angel would desire to visit, where an angel would seek to be a guest.* For it will bring the greater blessings, the greater glories, the greater contentment, the greater satisfaction; the glorious harmony of adjusting thyself and thy relationships one with another in making same ever harmonious. Do not begin with, "We will do it tomorrow—we will begin next week—we will make for such next year." Let that thou sowest in thy relationships day by day be the seeds of truth, of hope, that as they grow to fruition in thy relationships, as the days and the months and the years that are to come go by, they will grow into that garden of beauty that makes indeed for the home.

If ye have builded such that hate, envy, malice, jealousy are the fruits of same, these can only bring dissension and strife and hardships. *But if the seeds of truth and life are sown, then the fruition—as the life goes on together—will be in harmony.* And He, the Father, being thy guide in all will bless thee, even as He has promised from the beginning. *For in the fruit of thy bodies may many be blessed,* if ye will but seek that through the union of thy purposes, of thy desires, with their import in things spiritual, such may come to pass. (480–20)

Premarital Advice for a Male, Age Twenty-eight (lawyer, Hebrew): (939–1)

Q: Will the mental, physical, and spiritual interests of . . . and (939) be best served by their marriage to each other?
A: If their purposes, aims, desires are kept as held in the present, as we have indicated, these would best be suited one for the other.
Q: Are they prepared mentally, physically, and spiritually for marriage to each other?
A: Prepared.
Q: Do they genuinely love each other?
A: In the present. Remember each, love is giving; it is a growth. It may be cultivated or it may be seared. That of selflessness on the part of each is necessary. Remember, the union of body, mind, and spirit in such as marriage should ever be not for the desire of self but as *one.* Love grows; love endures; love forgiveth; love understands; love keeps those things rather as opportunities that to others would become hardships.

Then, do not sit *still* and expect the other to do all the giving, nor all the *for*giving; but make it rather as the unison and the purpose of each to be that which is a complement one to the other, ever.

Q: If they marry, will they be happy and compatible?
A: This, to be sure is a state that is *made* so: not a thing that exists. For life is living, and its changes that come must be met by each under such circumstances and conditions as to *make* the union, the associations, the activities, such as to be more and more worthwhile. Let each *ever* be dependent upon the other, yet so conducting self that the other may ever depend upon self. Thus will they find the associations, the mental forces,

the spiritual activities that will bring peace and contentment in such a union.

Q: If they marry, what course of conduct should each adopt toward the other to achieve greatest happiness and compatibility?

A: As has been indicated. One for the other, ever; more and more selfless when it comes to associations. This does not mean *either giving up;* but they each should express themselves as a complement to the best that is in each.

Q: If married, what activities and pursuits would they enjoy most in common?

A: Those that make for the preparing of themselves for being the complement one to the other. To be sure, in (939) it is necessary—with the associations in the legal phase of the experiences—of the entity and its development—that the service to others ever be a helpful hopefulness. But they should each budget their time for their daily expressions, their daily needs, their social activities, their developments in the mental, in the material, in the spiritual welfare.

These are the manners, the interests. As this: "What will prepare my mind the most to be on an equal footing with my husband, that the interests may be as one? So that when there are those things necessary for the more perfect understanding I would be able to meet him on his own ground?"

The same with the husband should be; not different worlds through their associations, socially, morally, or materially, but *ever* as a oneness of service, in a *constructive* manner ever.

Q: If they marry, will there be issue; and if so, how many boys and girls?

A: This would depend, to be sure, upon their activity in these relationships. Two as we find in the present; a girl, a boy—in that order.

Q: What knowledge of . . . and her personality does (939) require to aid him in understanding her?

A: Study rather not the whims or fancies that may be gratified, but that which would bring out the best in each. As (939) would for . . . as . . . would for (939). Study each other; not to become critical, but as to become more and more the complement one for the other.

Q: What knowledge of (939) and his personality does . . . require to aid her in understanding him?

A: The same. In the associations let them, as it were, each have their own jobs; yet *all* in common. Leave the office in the office, when in the home. Leave the petty things of the home in the home, when abroad. But have all things in common.

Q: Is (939) economically prepared to marry?

A: Prepared, to *meet* the conditions, provided they each take upon themselves their jobs to *meet* conditions and circumstances as they arise. (939-1)

Premarital Advice for a Female, Age Twenty (Protestant): (1722-1)

10/28/38 Letter: "I have been quite worried over the religious question in my coming marriage, and will be grateful for any help you can give me."

In giving advice and counsel in such conditions it is very well that the premise be given from which such conclusions are drawn for the advice and counsel.

Each soul in entering an earth's experience does so through the graciousness, the mercy of the living Father, that the soul may become such that it may be in that association, that relation to the Creative Forces or the Father which was, is, the will of the Father in bringing such into consciousness in the first or beginning.

In entering then, each soul enters with the influences both latent and manifested (emotions and attitudes) that have been a part of the experience of the entity. This to be sure includes then relationships with others.

Then what is the purpose of each soul's entering a material manifestation? That it may be a witness-bearer for and unto the glory of the Father which has been manifested through the Son, even Jesus: in making then these activities through and in which such may be the purpose, the desire of the individual entity.

It is not then that there may be the satisfying of the mental or material body, or mind. It is not to the indulgence of, nor to the glory of self alone, but that—through the very activities of the body and mind—the fruits of the spirit of truth may be manifested in the material experience.

These truths, these experiences, only find expression in relationships with others. Just as He hath given, "Inasmuch as ye have done it unto the least of these, thy brethren, ye have done it unto me—inasmuch as ye did NOT these things unto thy brethren, ye did them not unto me."

Hence in the relationships, the meetings with others in WHATEVER form or manner, such are not coincidental but are rather as purposeful experiences.

Look then into thine own heart, thine own mind. See thyself, as it were, pass by. What is thy desire? What is thy purpose? What—and WHO—is thy ideal?

The analysis of such can only be drawn by self. And use as the measuring stick of thyself those truths, those purposes.

What gave He as the whole law? To love thy God with all thy mind, thy body, thy purpose; and thy NEIGHBOR as thyself! This is the whole law.

And the manner of execution of same is in that as He gave, "As ye would that men should do to you, do ye even so to them."

These are the principles, these are the basic truths upon which joy, peace, and understanding may be thine; and thy life, thy activities, thy associations with others will ever be beautiful, peaceful, harmonious.

And as ye do these, ye will find more and more the glory of His presence abiding with thee day by day!

"Let my life be so filled with the desire to be a channel of blessings to others that it may show forth the Lord of Lords, the King of Kings." Ready for questions.

Q: I am practically engaged to the entity known as David. . . . Will our union be a spiritual, mental, and physical one?
A: If the choice, if the activity of each is given in such a way that you look to make of yourselves the ideal mate for the other. Not continually seeking or finding fault, either one with the other—but correcting the errors, the faults, the shortcomings in SELF; and ye will bring the best that is in self and make for the manifesting of the best that is in thy helpmate.

These are the manners, these are the ways that are His ways. And when other ways are used as of self-indulgence, self-purpose irrespective of the privileges, the duties, the opportunities of the other as well of self, then there come turmoils, divisions, and strife.

Q: He is a Catholic and I am a Protestant. Should I become a Catholic as his family require if we are to get married, or is there another solution to this problem?
A: Why should not self become a Catholic? Is there that which is abhorrent to self in the tenets, the opportunities, the privileges of Catholicism? [Cayce himself was a Protestant.]

There may be rules or regulations that have in thine own mental self been abused—or misconstrued—but if thy heart and purpose is right, then is this to keep each of you in that way in which each is serving the other and not the family. Remember, ye are marrying one man, NOT a family, NOT a church! Ye are to live in thy associations one with another the purposes, the desires to fill that place thy God, thy Saviour would have thee fill! What has been thy meditation? That ye may be a channel of blessings!

Q: What is the karmic tie in previous lives that is bringing David and me together?
A: This would be drawn only from a paralleling of the lives of these as experienced in former appearances. They are *not* chance, but a divine purpose being worked out. Be thou then in accord, and let Him—the Lord—have His way with each of thee.

Q: In what way can I help David—overcome certain difficulties, and in what way can I help myself with my difficulties?
A: In the way and manner as we have just indicated. By living the life to fill the married purpose in the experience one of the other. It cannot, it must not be a one-sided affair. Have the perfect understanding—what has been given by that as an ideal, who became the mother of the channel through which He came materially? "Thy God will be my God, thy people shall be my people!"

Q: In what way can I handle the "mother-in-law situation" so that our married life will be governed by ourselves?
A: That's the trouble too oft in self, "to handle." But so live rather thine own life that there are no question marks as to thy purpose, as to thy intent toward her son—and no questions of a problem. Thus may the situations, the conditions that arise oft in such be that thy own conscience does not condemn thee. Then ye are able to look every man, every woman in the face and say, "The Lord forgive thee—the Lord bless the."

Q: What have I come to work out during this life period?
A: Thy inconsistencies—at times; thy lack of the sufficient amount of "give and take." Or, "To be what I would wish others to be." We are through for the present. (1722-1)

KARMIC RELATIONS

(For a Catholic Male Writer, Age Twenty-eight) (849–12)

Mr. C: Yes, we have the body, the enquiring mind, (849); this we have had before, and some of those associations and relations that have existed between these entities.

In giving that which may be helpful to these in the present, as we find, and as we have given, there is much that may be accomplished by these in their association —if their efforts are put in the right direction.

Much, to be sure, has to be worked out; in their application of not indulgences, not dependencies, not laudation one towards another, but in patience, in tolerance, in love that is truly manifest between those that would show forth in their every relation these attributes in their combined effort toward their fellowman.

Then, these used or applied in these ways and manners will make for a union that is holy, that is acceptable to Him. Each soul has it share *not only of responsibility* one toward the other, *but of dependency* one upon the other.

Let both ever strive in their relationships, then, to become more and more a complement one to the other. And in this manner may there come to each a life experience more and more worthwhile. Then more and more may the beauties of purposefulness, of righteousness, of patience, of love, grow to be more beauteous, more worthwhile in the experience of each.

Periods will arise when due consideration must be given to each, in your outlook, your obligations, your purposes; but let each know this union of purpose must be ever in the light of that thy Father, thy God, thy Saviour, would have thee do!

Let the ideals ever be set, then, in Him. Then those periods of turmoil, of fears and doubts on the part of each, will become stepping-stones for a greater and greater love, a greater expression of His love.

In thy applications of the whole of purposefulness, let it never be just for self. Consider others, even as He. Yet in the applications, let them be as one. *Know that it is a fifty-fifty union. One should not always be forgiving and the other forgiven!* But let both in their own selves look to and for that which will make the experience, the association, and the union of purpose, more and more as an exemplification of His Spirit, His Love, His Blessings upon all that ye do; so living, so acting, that ye may make this as the real standard, the real experience, the real beginning of each becoming more and more, more and more worthwhile.

Let both assume the obligations; not merely as obligations, not as duties, alone, *but as loving opportunities* for each to be that helpmate to the other which will make a life of beauty, of joy; not only to selves but to others also. Ready for questions.

Q: What dangers should the couple look for in the married life?
A: As intimated or shown, both must be tolerant; yet both must realize their love for the other as a purposefulness in Him.

Beware then, in each, of self and self's interest irrespective of the other.

Q: Any advice as to children?
A: This should not be *under* two and a half to three years. (849–12)

PAST LIFE ASSOCIATIONS

(Husband and Wife) (2072–15)

For, as in the relationships ye have born in the earth as husband and wife, that which is the ideal as set by the Maker Himself is in those means in which there would be two manifesting as one in their hopes, in their fears, in their desires, in their aspirations.

This do, *and as ye have lived as father and daughter, as mother and son, as companions, as friends, as acquaintances, with differences, each with their own axe to grind, be patient, be tolerant one with another,* as ye would desire a father to be patient with a daughter, a mother to be patient with a son, as companions with the hopes of their desire bringing into existence into a material manifestation a channel, a body for the manifestation of a soul recently from God. Ready for questions.

Q: Did we know one another in our French incarnation?
A: Here we might give you a great deal of what has been intimated through these channels as to what the vibrations of nations, as individuals might mean. No, ye didn't know each as individuals in the French, otherwise you'd have been different in the present. Why? *There is that which is the spirit of France.* Don't ever get the idea that, even under the stress through which the nation of France is passing, it will be eliminated from the earth. *It is as one of the seven sins, as well as one of the twelve virtues in the human family.*

No, not acquainted with one another; acquainted with some of the doings but these weren't very pretty at times.

Q: Did we know one another in our Palestine incarnation?
A: Ye did. These were periods when ye each were a helpful influence, as may be indicated by analyzing closer the activities of each. For this was a period and an experience which rings true to each, as is intimated through the varied prophets of old, that which is builded by a nation or a certain portion of the land, think indeed what is meant by that spoken to Moses:

"Take off thy shoes, for the ground on which thou standest is holy." Why? *Did you ever try to analyze why that ye enter some places, some homes which are indeed homes and others, from the very feel, if ye are sensitive at all, there is confusion, there is anger,* there is abuse, of all those natures present in that house, not a home? Try this by entering a church and go from there to a jail and then go from the jail into the church —you will find it. *So it is with individuals as they have entered earthly experience in various spheres or periods. These were not by chance.* Think not that God doeth things haphazardly. For He hath not willed that any soul should perish, but has prepared a way.

Those, then, who hold animosity, hold grudges are building for themselves that which they must meet in confusion, in abuse of self, abuse of others, abuse of groups. It is not strange that, if ye have read how that all nations—strange that they were made nations—no. For there must be every type, else where would the opportunity come for those who seek to manifest God in the earth? It is indeed not strange there are even in the Protestant churches, Methodist, Christian, Baptist, Congregational or the what, but it is to meet the needs. *What is God? All things to all men that all might know Him. Not that one is better than the other.* These, as individuals chose one another as companions. For what? Because they fitted into such companionship, becoming more and more daily as one and as a complement as one, finding in the other that which would answer their needs. Just as an individual, seeking God, finds in self. He must have lots of water to wash his sins away and the other may do it with a drop, but the water and the blood must be there. So it is with these companions, finding in each, as in this experience, that each sought and found that which answer in the present that of prayer, of meditation, of that vibration in each which may be as healing to selves, as hope for others.

Q: What were our names in the Palestine period?

A: Ruth and what should be called in the present Alec—for he was a pretty smart aleck then!

Q: Were we Essenes in the Palestine period?

A: The names themselves imply it, yes. But remember the Essenes had the divisions, just as you will find that most churches have their groups and divisions; these were in opposite groups of the Essenes. One held to—that it can happen—the other that God makes it happen. Which comes first, the hen or the egg? As was implied in that same question.

Q: What were our activities as Essenes?

A: As is indicated, they were so divided, that comparing them together isn't well. And as to using in the present, don't fall out with each other because one wants to listen to Brahms and the other to Liszt.

Q: Were we close to the Master?

A: In purpose, yes, and who is my brother, who is my sister? He who doeth the will, that is the closest to the Master; He who doeth the will of the Father. (2072–15)

PAST LIFE INFLUENCE

(Husband and Wife—Influences on Children) (934–7)

Q: In what incarnations were we associated, and how, that have had to do with our present difficulties?

A: As just indicated, these parallels may be drawn from the information which has been given. Also the knowledge may be obtained in such a way and manner that it may either become as stumbling stones or stepping-stones for helpful forces.

However, the idea and ideal should be rather the problems that exist by that association in the present. *The greater influence, to be sure, arises from that as we have indicated, when there were those periods of the worshipfulness to the body-activity, the body-associations, the body-influence.* (Grecian incarnation.)

Thus it has been and is the problem of each in the present to prevent the satisfying, the gratifying of bodily influence or emotions which arise for the moment —or appetites, or influences.

And these—because of the periods, the worshipfulness towards material things as related to body-desire—are the problems of each in the present.

Then, so live, so act, in relationships one to another, and to those about you, that there may never be a question, either as to conduct or as to appetites, or as to those influences. For it will be found that the greater temptation to the offspring will be imbibing too freely of the cup!

Q: Considering present financial situation, should (934) remain here at Virginia Beach through the summer? If so, through what channels should employment be sought?
A: Never flee from, hinder self from, meeting self; provided purposes, desires, and hopes are safe in Him.

It would be very well for (934) to remain in the environ of Virginia Beach in the present season, PROVIDED there is determination—and not only the determining but the actual LIVING of that verbally expressed in the present as to the hopes, the desires, respecting that to be accomplished in this material plane.

But FIND self not in the gratifying for the moment, nor in appetites. *Not that anyone is to become goody-goody, but good FOR something!* that all may see, may know, that there IS the purpose, there IS that in which God has not chosen unwisely in giving this entity and its companion such a soul for development in this experience.

Let it be rather said that indeed they have realized their privilege, their opportunity, to conduct their own

lives that they may be an example for this entity, this
soul. (934-7)

MARITAL RELATIONSHIPS—OBLIGATIONS
AND SUSPICIONS

(For a Female Protestant Housewife, Age Thirty-six)
(585-1)

In considering the conditions that exist in the marital,
physical, and material relations, that there may be
peace, harmony, and the fulfilling of the duties, obligations, morally, mentally, spiritually, that should exist in the home: all conditions should be taken into
consideration; as to what the home and relations are
a manifestation of in relationship to the home, the social surroundings, and the spiritual representations
that should be manifest there.

In the attitudes of self, then, there should not be contention in any manner, nor the producing or causing
by word or act that which brings contention of *any*
nature. This does not signify that one should counte-
nance or give moral support by not speaking when
there are indications of those relations being such as
to not be in keeping with that the home and such relations signify; for when such relations do not produce
that which is constructive and creative of mental and
spiritual relations, or that which is constructive and
creative of the higher or better or *good* relations, then
sin lieth at the door of someone.

The attitude should be rather in loving action and
word that the differences be pointed out, rather than
by contention, abuse, or any word or act that condemns anyone for their activity that would bring detrimental forces to action in such relations.

*Then, there should also be the pointing out of the
moral, material, and physical obligations that each*

*should bear one toward another, and when such has
failed wholly on the part of self or another there
should be then the activity as in relation to the physical obligations;* then when this has failed, prepare self
for what may ensue by the activities of others. These
as we find, though, carried forward in a manner that
will not produce contention but will bring peace, harmony, and an understanding that will make for the
better relationships in every sense. Ready for questions.

Q: Outline a specific method whereby I can get truth
over to my husband.
A: This is better by the mode of example than by precept, and these combined will move *any* thinking body
to the responsibility, obligation, moral fortitude, and
material relationships.
Q: Is there anything I have done, consciously or unconsciously, to bring about this condition?
A: This should best be answered in self, through those
conversations that should be had in bringing about the
understandings in those relationships that exist; knowing that in self if there is not lost that patience, fortitude, hope, faith, then the acts and words will be
guided by that which will bring about the better and
closer relationship. If these are lost, then self becomes
the one abused. The pointing out should be the abuse
that the other person is making in himself by the attitude and activities, and that in the abuse of self, self's
relationships, self's privileges, self's moral attitude, the
damage and wrong is done to himself and to those obligations that go with same!
Q: [She desired this question be left out of her copy.]
Am I correct in my suspicions of the certain women
involved?
A: This we would not give; for this is already condemning—without there being other than suspicion.
(585-1)

REPUTATION—ASSOCIATIONS

(Husband and Wife) (903–17)

Having chosen then whom ye shall serve—whether self, and the gratification of self's desires, or those obligations that have been assumed of self, those that have been given into thine keeping—let each, with that as is the answer—as in water the face answers to face—that which is known in self as the manner of *every* act, be guided accordingly. For, the answer is in self, and not for any moralist—or any wagging tongue that may seek to find fault, or that may spread any unkind word.

Q: In reference to (257), his personal affairs and conditions at home, please advise him whether he is right as to the proper conduct and relations with social conditions.
A: As given, judge ye from that which has already been set before thee! Thou knowest in self! But he that condemns is condemned already!
Q: Advise (903) her proper attitude as to being seen in public unaccompanied by her husband but with strangers.
A: As ye have chosen, and as ye choose—that which ye would have done to you, do ye even so to others!
Q: What will be public reaction as to her standing or danger of criticism?
A: Dare to do that that is right, and in accord with that ideal chosen as the standard for the home! Not what others will say, but—what is thine ideal? What would ye have said of self? What would ye say in the same circumstance? What is thy ideal? So act, so conduct self, *irrespective* of what others may say or others may do! Be rather as he of old, "Others may do as they may, but as for me and my house *we* will serve the living God!"

Q: Can she, being a mother, afford to risk her reputation by public appearances with other men when her husband is out of the city?

A: This, as we have intimated and given, shall be a cooperative decision; and this must be chosen of themselves, not from here! Is it directed, or is it right, that *any* should interfere? Or do other than, even as He has given, "As you sow, so shall ye reap—and men do not gather figs from thistles."

Q: Or, is (257) wrong in old ideas of associations?

A: *Who is able to judge as to what is the right or the wrong, save that a home, a haven, a heaven, must present and produce peace, harmony, understanding!* Then, let *each* conduct their lives in such a manner as befits that chosen as the ideal cooperation of each, as to their relationships to self, to each other, to home, and to their social surroundings. (903–17)

DOMESTIC STRIFE—DIVORCE

(For a Female Protestant Bookkeeper, Age Thirty-seven) (845)

First, as we find, there must be at this time the due consideration given as respecting the own physical and mental experiences.

True, an individual, a soul, must become less and less of self—or thoughts of self; yet when those activities of others in *relationships* to the mental, the spiritual, the *soul* developments are such that the own soul development and own soul expression becoming in jeopardy, *then, as He hath given, "I came not to bring peace but a sword. I came to give peace, not as the world counts peace,"* but as that which makes for those experiences *wherein the soul, the entity, is to fulfill those purposes, those activities, for which it—the soul-entity—came into being.*

And when those relationships about same have been and are such that those conditions arise wherein there is the lack of harmonious effects that are possible, *then as He hath given, put at naught those experiences, those influences. Let them be rather as they were not.* (Loving indifference. See Chapter X.)

In the physical forces of the body there needs be *rest,* there needs be relief from physical, mental anxieties. *For these continue in the present to make for that influence wherein the very vitality, the very life existence is being put into that position of where there is the rebellion between the spiritual, the mental, the material, and the mental; and these make for such physical anxieties between the material forces and the soul forces that they rebel one with another.*

These then are as conditions in all the relationships, in the home, in the associations, in the domestic relations, in the activities. Whatever thy choice is, let these be ever with an eye single to service to that living influence of being a better, a greater channel of blessings to someone.

Not of self—choosing an easier way; not of self attempting to escape that as is necessary for thine own understanding, thine own soul development; but rather ever, "Thy will, O Lord, be done in and through me. Use me as Thou seest I have need of, that I may be a *living* example of thy love, of thy guidance in this material experience." Ready for questions.

Q: Should I break up housekeeping, board, or share expenses with those now in my household?
A: This would depend upon the choices that are made. *Remember you are meeting self.* In whatever choice is made, face the issues in thine own life, in those with whom you may be associated. For those problems that are thy problems are others' problems. Meet them as is befitting that as is *shown* thee in thine inner self. Loneliness is destructive, yet in *Him* ye may find companionship. We are through for the present.

FAMILY RELATIONSHIPS

(For a Female, Said to Have Been in Palestine as "The Woman Accused of Adultery.") (1436-3)

Q: Would it be best to remain in the same apartment with my family for the present or try to borrow money enough to get a place for myself?
A: It would be better to remain. If the environ is such that not only self is antagonistic to the family, or the family so antagonistic to the body but the self continuing to be antagonistic, then change. But if there is sought by the entity for not the differences that exist in the minds of the family and the associations but as to how the entity may be a help to those in the family in finding THEIR relationships to Creative Forces, this will make for the better surroundings, making the security of the entity in its abilities for stabilizing itself in a much surer and a much better means or manner.

Separation would leave not only a grudge and an animosity and a feeling of spitefulness on the part of self but on the part of the family such as to build that which ye have learned or been taught to call KARMA.

In the mental and spiritual self and direction it has been shown thee how ye have gained, through those very activities by contact with LIFE ITSELF; how animosities, grudges, feelings of differentiations or the evaluation of activities in the experience must be—as in the present experience and associations—a PRACTICAL application of same.

To have the feeling of aloofness because of variations in the thoughts of the associations of the mental self, without consideration as to how the very conditions are brought about for the usefulness of all, is to lose sight of the very evaluation or activity of truth IN the experience of self!

Then as we find, if there is gained the proper insight from the information given as respecting the physical and mental and spiritual self, the application of same would be in the home or in that environ of same.

Q: *Is there some karmic debt to be worked out* with either or both (father and brother) and should I stay with them until I have made them feel more kindly toward me?

A: These— *What IS karmic debt? This ye have made a bugaboo! This ye have overbalanced within thyself! What is thy life but the gift of thy Maker that ye may be wholly one with Him?*

Thy relationships to thy fellows through the various experiences in the earth come to be then in the light of what Creative Forces would be in thy relationships to the ACT ITSELF! And whether it be as individual activities to those who have individualized as thy father, thy mother, thy brother or the like, or others, it is *merely self being MET,* in relationships to that they *THEMSELVES* are working out *and not a karmic debt BETWEEN but a karmic debt of SELF that may be worked out BETWEEN the associations that exist in the present! And this is true for every soul.* If ye will but take that as was given *thee,* "Neither do I condemn thee—neither do I condemn thee."

WHO GAVE THAT? *LIFE ITSELF!* Not a personality, not an individual alone; though individually spoken to the entity, to the soul that manifests itself in the present in the name called (1436). This becomes then not an incident but as a LESSON, that ALL may learn: That is the reason, that is the purpose, that is why in the activity much should be expected, why much shall be endured, why much may be given, by the soul that has learned that God condemns not they that seek to know His face and BELIEVE!

Then it is not karma but in HIM that the debt is paid.

For who forgave thee thy material shortcomings, thy material errors, as judged by thy superiors at that experience in the material world?

Thy Lord, thy Master—THYSELF! For He stands in thy stead, before that WILLINGNESS of thy inner self; thy soul, to do good unto others; that willingness, that seeking is righteousness, if ye will but understand, if ye will but SEE—and FORGET the LAW that killeth (the wages of sin is Death!) but remember the spirit of forgiveness that makes alive! (1436-3)

COMPANIONSHIP

For God hast given thee a wonderful opportunity in the companionship of thy foster mother. While not too many years will be granted thee in that companionship, make good while ye may, else there will come periods of regret, and such regrets become as (a) canker to the mind and body. (5049-1)

CHILD GUIDANCE

(For a Male, Age One, Said to Have Been Stephen Foster)

EC: Yes, we have the records here of that entity now called (5306).

In giving the interpretations of that as we find, much more of this should be given to those who are responsible for the entity's advent into the material world, and as to what then may be expected of the entity, and warnings as to how those who are responsible shall environ the entity for greater unfoldment.

As we have indicated for others, those entering the material plane in '43, '44, '45, '46 are purposeful individual entities, and much will depend upon these souls as to what manner of activity will be in the world a score of years hence.

The general tendency of this entity is to be first stubborn; not that the will of the entity should be broken, yet these should be as tenets and truths lived by those about the entity, rather than precepts of, "You do this because I say this, you do this because Uncle John thinks it's right or Aunt Jane says you ought to do this."

Don't say one thing in the presence of the child and do something else yourself. Don't give instructions or ask the child to do that which you do not do yourself, for you yourself become a liar in the very act of same.

Do make for the principle of the teachings of love, patience, gentleness, kindness. These, as ye manifest them in his presence, will bring to the formation of ideals.

There will be the tendency towards music, as will be seen from some appearances, though just a few may be given in the present, and then when ye have done something about those possibilities in music, in verse, in song, there may be those others given which may be the more helpful for this entity.

As to the appearances of the entity in the earth, as indicated, only the one before this may be given in the present:

For the entity then was of the song writers whose words and music were of the type which has lived and will live longer than any one individual American.

So, the entity will be so American as to be hard to get along with, even when other lands or names are mentioned, during the first twelve years of its sojourn in the earth.

For the entity was Stephen C. Foster, and how little others then thought of the entity and now how much he is thought of, but few still appreciate the abilities.

Hates will be easy for the entity, because of the slights and the slurs which were parts of the experience.

Evenness of temper will be those things to bring into the experience, through the gentleness, through the patience, manifested.

And when the entity is some ten to twelve years of age, we will give the connections with others. (Suggestion for a future life reading. E.C. did not live another ten years.)

Remember, those responsible for the entity must instruct; not Aunt Sue or Aunt Emily or Uncle John, but the father and mother. There the responsibility lies. We are through, then, for the present. (5306-1)

CHILD GUIDANCE (59-12)

Q: Give father (257) specific guidance as to how he can direct this child.
A: Study first in self (the father) to show self approved unto its ideals and *not* to *tradition!* "For of tradition," as the Lord hath given, "I AM DONE!" But with purposefulness of knowing and giving the better reaction.

For as the developing mind is reaching that with its studies, its readings, towards hero worship—unless self (the father or the mother) can *remain* the hero, you fail in meeting the full needs of the developing mind.

This is done then first in showing self approved unto that which is the ideal in spirituality, in self! And let that be rather the guide, ever, in *forming* the relationships, the associations in the daily life.

For remember, the mind and the body is a growing thing. GROW with same! Unless that growth is apparent, then the parent becomes to the growing mind a "back number," and out of date.

Hence the parents should grow with, be companionable with, cooperate with, all the surroundings.

To deny the daily activities, the daily instruction in school as being passé or forward is to create a barrier between the child and the parent. All must be then cooperative.

To deny or to build a barrier between one parent and another in its correction, then this again builds a barrier. And they (the children) cannot love two masters. They (the parents) must be ONE!

Well that the world would learn that given of old, "Know O Israel (O Parents), the Lord thy God is ONE!"

And unless the purpose of all those that aid, all those that guide, all those that direct the developing life of a soul are ONE, they build destructive forces in its (the soul's) experience.

Not that problems do not arise in the experience of each: the father, the child, the mother, the instructor. Yet ever if these are as ONE, His promises—God's promises—*become* effective.

Yet if there is the attempt—as has been indicated—to have *self's* way (the egotism, the self-expression), ye defeat the First Law.

Q: Should he be forbidden to play with fire, or should that curiosity be directed—if so, how?

A: This is an element (fire), and an elemental, and an experience in the activity of every individual. *The entity then must learn its lesson. Take in consideration that as has been given. Forbidding creates a barrier.* Then *direction as* to its purposes, as to it benefits, as to its place in the experience of every soul is necessary. But as a toy, as a plaything, this then becomes taboo; and should be handled, should be directed.

Forbidding in the life of *this* entity, as in most others, becomes—WHAT TEMPTATION! (759–12)

GUIDANCE—MOTHER AND SON—PHYSICAL IMBALANCES

(For a Male, Age Twenty) (830-2)

Mr. C.: Yes, we have the body, the inquiring mind (811), and the body, the inquiring mind of (830).

In counseling with an individual entity there are many conditions that are to be taken into consideration.

While the desire of the mother to aid is natural, is right, there must be the realization that the individual has his own life to live—and that even the great desire to aid may at times become a stumbling block to another individual.

Then the greater aid is to counsel as respecting his purpose, his ideal. *For each soul enters the material plane for the manifesting of its individual application of an ideal in respect to the Creative Forces or Energies.* (Note the emphasis on an individual's application to its own ideal.)

Each soul is then endowed by its Maker with that of choice, with that birthright. And to live another's life, and to direct or counsel even—other than that which is in accord with that of choice—is to become rather a hindrance than an aid.

For there are no short cuts to knowledge, to wisdom, to understanding—these must be lived, must be experienced by each and every soul.

In counsel then, let thy yeas be yea and thy nays be nay.

The anxiety that has arisen in self has only unfit self, as well as oft brought confusion in the experience of the individual—the son; with the desire not to be averse to filling the requirements for the peace, the harmony—yet these bring oft to the entity confusions.

Q: Why is he unable to sit still and study?
A: A physical disturbance oft becomes the condition, and yet being under those adverse influences—the desires of the body to be active, to be creative in its own self override same; and combined with those pressures the hindrances become rather in the body being quiet or still.

These are not faults, but rather than *use* them as stepping-stones for the better approach. HAVE the physical corrections made but *do not* attempt to INSIST that there must be quiet! For it merely creates then that subjugation of the WILL; and the will once broken, the will once disturbed to that, it becomes rather that of a defiance.

For each soul, each mind, each entity is endowed with its choice. And the choice is the result of the application of self in relationships to that which is its ideal—and finds manifestation in what individuals call habit, or subconscious activity. Yet it has its inception in that of choice.

For to subjugate an individual soul to the will of another is to break that which is the greater power, the greater influence in the experience of the soul for its advancement. Consider for the moment, then, the desires, the promptings in the body, the mind, the soul of (830).

Because the physical defects or suppressions in the body through those areas that affect the pineal and the adrenals are existent, then there are hindrances in the body's being able to fulfill even that as is innate and a desire. *For to be an architect or an engineer of such and such varied activities is innate, yet to force self to the rote, to the necessary requirements, becomes to the entity oft as unbearable experiences;* and it reaches at times those expressions in self that, "It isn't worth the effort." He would rather chuck the whole thing and just drift with the tide.

Then through corrective mechanical applications have those corrections made, and then if the corrections are such that the choice of the entity can be and is in those directions that have been indicated—well! If those activities then are such yet that the choice must be made of its own in the physical or material applications, in labors that find an outlet for the activities, let the *entity* choose! *Do not force!*

Hence it behooves those who are interested, those who have the welfare of this entity upon their hearts and souls, to first through the *physical* means make as much reparation as possible.

But still in prayer, in thought, in desire; but not constantly picking at or suggesting or finding fault. For has thy Father, thy God, found fault with thee? Hath He not blessed thee rather in every undertaking; whether in those directions that were holy or partially or entirely opposed to His will? Be thou greater than He?

Give of thy love, give of thy patience, give of thy long-suffering. For that ye *give*, that ye possess! That ye spend in arguments, in suggestions that are self-centered, ye never possess, ye never retain.

Do thy part; thy Maker will do His.

Q: What was the reason for his lack of success in his studies at VPI, the school suggested in his Life Reading?
A: As has been indicated, the lack of the ability—through physical disturbance—to concentrate. Not that there wasn't the consecration—but to concentrate! For the disturbance and the surroundings made for rather confusion.
Q: What is suggested for him to do now?
A: First we would have those physical corrections, as indicated, and then the choice must be made by the entity; as to whether it will so train, so rule, so govern

self as to prepare its way for that as is innate, or as to whether the preparation will come through physical application in labor, in work.

Q: Are his living conditions all right?

A: The adjustments of every individual, with an *ideal*, may ever fit him for *whatever* surroundings there may be. Hence the advice, the counsel, is to KNOW SELF and WHAT *IS* THY IDEAL! Not in WHO or in what.

[Repeated] "While the desire of the mother to aid is natural, is right, there must be the realization that the individual has his own life to live—and that even the great desire to aid may at times become as a stumbling block to another individual." (830–2)

CONCEPTION—PARENTAL ATTITUDES

(For a Female, Age Thirty-four) (457–11)

As has been indicated, as may be read by the body, and as the body may know in those experiences of Sarah, Rachel, and Hannah, conception is a gift of God; it should ever be considered such.

And with such ideals may the body make itself a fit channel, and not merely considering it as of a physical act. Ready for questions.

Q: Why has conception not taken place?

A: Ask self! For, in the light of such as we have just indicated, only in self may the answer come. Has God seen fit to give thee that thou seekest? Hast thou prepared thyself as a worthy channel of His consideration? Only self may answer.

Q: Was there not enough time allowed before the menstruation?

A: This is not a matter of purely a physical act. Do not consider same from that angle alone; else it will be to thine own undoing.

Q: Is there any way to tell when the flow from the ovary is taking place?

A: Not as yet has such been discovered. This may only be given by the grace and mercy of God. True, it is a pathological condition, that through certain periods or times takes place—this is a law of nature. Conception is a law of God.

Q: Is it not important to know the time that conception takes place?

A: This may not be known until there has been sufficient time for the meeting of the sperm and the activities in the body of self; and this only by the pathological effect created.

Q: Is it the general purpose of the parents all the time that is important and the moment that conception takes place doesn't make any difference?

A: This is considering such only from a physical angle, and it is not such at all—if a body is to be a worthy channel for one of His own.

Q: Also the attitude, is it important at moment of conception or rather the daily and continuous attitude of both parents?

A: Attitude is as necessary as the act itself.

Q: Does the semen have any direct effect on the physical body of the woman? Is it absorbed by the body.

A: No. It only has effect upon the ovum, and that brings about—from a physical standpoint—conception. Only when it is pierced by same.

Q: Does the douche of bicarbonate of soda before intercourse have any effect on the sex of the child?

A: The sex of the child depends upon the attitudes of the individuals, and especially those held by the mother. As to whether it is the male or female oft may depend upon the discharge of the opposite sex. That of them other brings the son; that of the father brings the daughter. They are opposites.

Q: Is the sex of a child determined at conception or developed later?

A: It may be determined at least six to ten years after birth, in some instances. Hence it is not at conception, but dependent upon the growth or the cycle of that vibration set about that produces the conception.

Q: Is it wrong for mankind to seek a way of determining the sex of a child?

A: Depends upon what he does with it. *Knowledge of itself is not wrong; it is the application of same that becomes sin.* (457–11)

SEX EDUCATION—SEX RELATIONS— GENERAL

(For a Male, Age Thirty-four, Lawyer, Protestant) (826–6)

Mr. C.: Yes, we have the inquiring mind of (826), also those desires of presenting the conditions as timely warnings for the young in this age and this experience.

As we find, in presenting what may be helpful in the education way and manner, as we have indicated, *the condition that exists in the present* as related to the relationships in sex—or the greater cause for the lack of judgment, the lack of proper consideration, the lack of those things necessary to prevent the laxness and the practice of those conditions and experiences as related to same—*is from the lack of education in the young before their teen-age years!*

For few there be who have the proper understanding, as we have indicated, of what the biological urge produces in the body!

Now whether such an education is to be undertaken in the home or in the school is the greater problem.

To be sure, there are conditions existent in relationship to man of the denominational activities religiously that prohibit, bar, or prevent sufficient consideration of these problems in the public schools or even in the private schools.

And little has there been of the proper education of the mother, the father of those who need such instruction.

But these are the places to begin. And the warnings as would be presented are *not* as to the practices of this or the manner of that, or the association of this or that in the adult life. But there should be those precautions, understandings, relationships as to how and in what manner there becomes the biological urge; which through the proper training may become a *pathological* condition in the body of the individual. *For it is as from the beginning of puberty the essence of the Creative Forces or Energies* (manifests) *within the body of the individual.*

And if such forces are turned to those channels for the aggrandizement of selfish motives, or the satisfying of that within the urge for the gratification of emotions, they become destructive; not only in the manner of the offspring but also in the very *physical body* of the offspring, as well as in the energies of the bodies so producing same.

These are the approaches that *should* be given as timely warnings to the mother, the father; and as for the *young* these should be rather as the suggestions for the instructors, the warnings to the parents as to the conversation of the nurse, the maid, or as to the exercisings of the children in their formative years— in *whatever* relationships there may be.

And then, as these grow and become a portion of the politic body for public education, there should be the greater stress laid upon the educations in these directions; and not wait until they have reached or arrived at that position where they begin to study physiology, anatomy, or hygiene. *But even in the formative years there should be the training in these directions,* as a portion of the material things. Even as the child studies its letters, let a portion of the instructions be in the care of the body, and more and more in the stress upon the care in relation to the sex of the body and in the preservation of that as to its relationships to its Creator.

For it is through such factors, through such bodies of activity, that there may become a manifestation of the spiritual forces such as to bring *into being* those of one's own flesh and blood.

These are the approaches. These are the conditions.

Do not begin halfway. *Do not begin after there has been already begun the practice of the conditions that make for destructive forces,* or for the issue of the body to become as a burning within the very elements of the body itself—and to find expression in the gratifying of the emotions of the body!

For, to be sure, relationships in the sex are the exercising of the highest emotions in which a physical body may indulge. And only in man is there found that such are used as that of destruction to the body-offspring! This, then, is the approach; this is the manner. Ready for questions.

Q: Is monogamy the best form of home relationship?
A: Let the teachings be rather toward the spiritual intent. Whether it's monogamy, polygamy, or what not, let it be the answering of the spiritual *within* the individual!

But monogamy is the best, of course, as indicated from the scripture itself—*One—ONE!* For the union of one should ever be *one.*

Q: Is marriage as we have it necessary and advisable?
A: It is!
Q: Should divorces be encouraged by making them easier to obtain?
A: This depends upon first the education of the body. Once united, once understood that the relationships are to be as one, less and less is there the necessity of such conditions. *Man may learn a great deal from a study of the goose in this direction. Once it has mated, never is there a mating with any other—either the male or female, no matter how soon the destruction of the mate may occur—unless forced by man's intervention.*

This does not indicate that this is the *end* and should *only* remain as such. For, as we have indicated, *this* is indicated by the name and the *meaning* of the name itself. For this is the *extreme*. Just as indicated in all of the animals—the fowl or those that have become the closer related to man, and man's intervention in their surroundings and their activities and their adaptabilities; in their *natural* state these are in the forms as their *names* indicate. And from these man may learn many lessons; which *was* attempted in the beginning. And yet, as we have indicated, in same he lost self in that he found that he could satisfy those emotions or *gratify* what might be builded as emotions from experience to experience.

Thus there were gradually brought on the various polygamous relationships that have existed through-out the ages in many periods. And, as indicated in the lives of groups and nations, these become the stum-bling blocks that are ever kept within the background —but that have made for the destructive influence that arose within the activities of such groups and nations, in such relationships.

Hence to begin, begin with the *Mind*. For, as we have said, to build the perfect relationship in *any* direction that there may be brought a union is to begin before the parents of such are born! In *their* own minds!

Hence to begin with the teen age, or at twenty, or at fifty, or with an older individual, is only to have the tail end of something! and does not tend to be con-structive at all! Only does it become a form.

But begin with those when they are *choosing* their mate, see?

Q: Should nudism be encouraged?
A: That should be a matter of principle within the individuals as there is the training as to what is the purpose of those parts covered. Nudism or clothing or whatnot, as we have *oft* indicated, should be *rather*

the matter of the environ—and not a matter of moral principle in *any* sense!

Q: Is the broadcasting of birth control information advantageous in improving the race?

A: *It is like shooting feathers at an eagle!* It's a move in the right direction, but that's about as much as might be said. This should be rather the *training* of those that are in the positions of *being* the mothers and fathers *of* the nation, of the peoples!

What are the factors in the lives of those that broadcast such? Look into those and ye may easily find the answer to your question. Not all, but *most* are prompted by something that is lacking in their *own* makeup.

Who giveth the increase? Man may plant, man may sow. Man understanding, then, the varied activities of a given condition—through the education in the character of the soil, in the elements going to make up the body of that sought to be produced—*prepares* for same. But who giveth the increase? *Who* maketh for that which it arises?

So with the education, so with that which does the prompting, let it be from not that which is *lacking* in an urge, but rather from *what* is to be done by the individual *with* the urge! See? And leave the results with the *Giver* of Life!

For Life is of, and is, the Creative Force; it is that ye worship as God.

Those then that besmirch same by overindulgence besmirch that which is best within themselves. And that should be the key to birth control or sex relations, or every phase of the relationships between the sons and the daughters of men—that would become the Sons and Daughters of God.

Q: Is continence in marriage advisable except when mating to produce offspring?

A: This should be, and is, as we have indicated in the

matter of education, the *outcome* of the *universal* sources of supply of the individuals. For some, yes; in other cases it would be *very* bad on the part of each, while in others it would be bad on one, or the other, see?

There should be, then, rather the educating as to the *purposes*, and how, HOW that the force, the vitality, that goes for the gratifying of emotions may be centralized in creating—in the lives of others about the body in all its various phases—spiritual blessings.

Q: Should men or women who do not have the opportunity to marry have sex relationships outside of marriage?
A: This again is a matter of principle within the individual. The sex organs, the sex demands of every individual, must be gratified in *some* manner as a portion of the biological urge within the individual. These *begin* in the present with curiosity. *For it is as natural for there to be sexual relations between man and woman, when drawn together in their regular relations or activities, as it is for the flowers to bloom in the spring,* or for the snows to come in the winter, when the atmospheric conditions are conducive or inducive to such conditions.

When a man or woman has chosen (for it must be choice, and is only by choice that one remains out of relationships with the opposite sex in marriage)—if it has chosen to not be in such relationships, then be true to the choice; or else it is to self a sin! For that which one would pretend to be and isn't is indeed sin!

Q: Should they raise children outside of marriage?
A: It answers itself.
Q: Would it be better for a woman, who desires to marry, to be one of two or mores wives to a man in a home rather than to remain unmarried?
A: This is again a matter of *principle;* or the urge within such conditions must be conformative to that set as the ideal.

In the education of individuals as regarding sex relationships, as in every other educational activity, there must be a standard or a rule to go by or an ideal state that has its inception not in the emotions of a physical body but from the spiritual ideal which has been set, which was set and given to man in his relation to the Creative Forces.

Then to ask or to seek or to advise or to give suggestions even, that it may be done outside of that, isn't being true to that as is presented. We are through for the present. (826–6)

Chapter VII

Balanced Living: The Problem of Extremes

For if thine eye be single—then thy WHOLE BODY is full of light. But if ye are attempting to have the physical body doing just as IT PLEASES, the mental body controlled by "What will other people say?", and thy spiritual body and mind shelved only for good occasions and for the good impressions that you may make occasionally, there CANNOT BE other than confusion. (5246)

We find that these ailments arose as a result of what might be called occupational disturbances: not enough in the sun, not enough of hard work. Plenty of brain work. But the body is supposed to coordinate the spiritual, mental and physical. (3352)

But keep a normal balance, not by being an extremist in any direction—whether in diet, exercise, spirituality, or mentality—but in all let there be a coordinance influence. For, every phase of the physical, mental, and spiritual life is dependent upon the other. They are as one—as the Father-God is one. (2533–3)

Q: What should be my procedure to hasten my spiritual and mental development?

A: Make haste here slowly, for this—the spiritual and mental—is as a growth. Ye GROW in grace, in knowledge, in understanding and as the application is made daily in thy relationships to others, so is the growth accomplished. (510)

As to speeding same—make haste slowly. Remember that overenthusiasm is as bad as dilatory activity. Great movements, great forces, move slowly. (1151–21)

Q: Have personal vices as tobacco and whiskey any influence on one's health or longevity?
A: As just has been indicated, you are suffering from the use of some of these in the present, but it is over-indulgence. *In moderation these are not too bad, but man so seldom will be moderate.* (5233–1)

Much of man's problem in the earth stems from the fact, noted in the above readings, that he will not be moderate, individually or collectively. The readings continually affirm that moderation is a balanced condition of great value, worthy of our consideration and efforts toward attainment. The key word in considering moderation versus extremism is, of course, "BALANCE"—the meeting of opposites or extremes—and as we've noted, the readings state that only in Christ Jesus is there the meeting of the extremes.

All biological life as we know it, from single-celled protozoans to multicellular man, is an expression of living protoplasm—continually moving, acting, and reacting in an attempt to maintain an internal and external balance with the environment. Our bodies must constantly function in a manner which attempts to achieve balance. If the temperature is hot, we perspire, if cold, we shiver. In order to move our bones, one set of muscles must contract and an opposing set relax. Even the physically inert portions of creation balance themselves and necessarily so for us, for if liquids and gases did not diffuse in an effort to achieve a balance in pressure, then osmosis would cease and all living cells would die, polluted by their own self-poisoning excretions.

The problem of the balance of nature and earth's present ecological condition is another prime example of man's extremism in pursuit of self-interests, with disastrous effects. Even the astrological aspects of the readings make note of these implications by pointing to Uranus as the planet of extremes. Uranus, ruler of Aquarius, heralded the Industrial Revolution and more recently the atomic age (Uranium) which has so violently upset the balance of nature and political activity in the earth. Uranus will have been in Libra, the sign of balance, until 1974–75, when it moves to Scorpio for the next seven years (December, 1981). Scorpio signifies among other things, death and rebirth, decay and regeneration, so that with Uranus transiting it till 1982 the choice set before us will be made clear, "Life or death, good or evil. Choose whom ye would serve." The portents seem ominous, particularly when we reflect on the individual's helplessness to eradicate social ills, crime and violence, warfare, global pollution, poverty, mental illness—and disease.

The problems are immense and we are so small as to be completely overwhelmed by the contrast. Yet the readings note that individually we are not only part of the whole of Creation, but that our minds, individually, encompass all of the universe.

The readings further suggest, in concurrence with much philosophic thought, that if one would change the world, one must first perfect self—or at least begin with some movement in that direction. Balance is again the keynote: "That which is so hard to understand in the minds or experiences of many is that the activities of a soul are for self-development yit (the soul) must be selfless in its activity, for it, the soul, to develop." (275–39)

The balance here is self versus selflessness as the crux of personal attitude. Having previously touched upon extremes in mental attitudes we would now have you consider extremes within the physical body itself, remembering that, "The body is the temple of the Living God," and the promise is "within the temple He will meet thee" —or, "All we may know of heaven or hell is within our own selves."

BODY BALANCE

The human body is truly a remarkable mechanism. Mystics have compared it in microcism to the entire universe, and the readings liken each of us as unto "corpuscles in the body of God." The human body not only contains portions of every element found in the earth, but according to the readings each cell is a universe in itself, having a consciousness of its own. This cellular consciousness intermingles and is closely associated with the autonomic nervous system. Most of the various body balances are maintained and directed in this fashion. Growth, organic activity and maintenance, protection and repair are carried on automatically by the individual cells of the body in cooperation with the whole.

For example, if a pregnant mother's diet is deficient in calcium, the body will "borrow" it from the mother's bones and teeth, parceling it off to the embryo. If an individual takes up an activity such as distance running or swimming, the body reacts to its own increased demand for oxygen and blood by not only increasing the size and strength of lungs and heart, but also by raising the efficiency ratio of oxygen needed to perform a given amount of work. Should a part of the body be bruised, cut, or attacked by disease bacteria the entire body reacts in defense, swelling to isolate the problem area, raising the white cell population in the blood (particularly concentrated at the point of trauma) plus an overall rise in body temperature and a general lethargic reaction by the body as a whole—all in a concerted cooperative effort to protect the balance of life.

Our autonomic nervous system and interconnecting cell consciousness maintains or attempts to maintain a balance in all body functions: respiration, circulation, digestion, assimilation, excretion, body weight and temperature, sleep, muscle tone, fluid balance, etc. Other important balances affected are:

Energy/vitality
Acid/alkaline
Oxygen/carbon dioxide
Vitamin/mineral
Enzymes/hormones

The body can manage to survive in spite of a great deal of imbalance within its basic structure and physiology. But at the same time it is very difficult to achieve spiritual growth or attunement when confronted with a throbbing headache or toothache, violent nausea or muscular cramps, chills, fever, chronic pain or irritability, etc.

Consequently, it is particularly significant that almost all of the people who sought out Edgar Cayce for readings did so initially because of personal illness, with little thought of spiritual matters or personal growth. In the same vein, much of Jesus' ministry was involved with healing the sick—who also came to Him with little interest in things spiritual. The immediate concern of most of us when we become ill *is Self*. (Which in perverse fashion is how we get sick in the first place!)

What we are intimating here is that our illnesses and imbalances seem to serve as bait—enticing our soul's awareness to surface and confront the conscious mind with inner truths which cry out for attention as the possible prelude to our spiritual awakenings. And while it is still no easier for us to pray or meditate during a prolonged coughing or choking spell than it is to sit attentively through a church service while in the throes of a dreadful physical/emotional hangover, the imbalances still will rankle us to attend them and ultimately seek some resolution.

Insofar as these body imbalances serve as a basis in our understanding, we should ask ourselves what primary imbalances or extremes we may have—or how do we shape up, healthwise, in the following regards?

1. Body weight—over/under?
2. Skeletal structure—posture, alignment, flexibility.
3. Nervous system—tension, lethargy, pain, irritability.
4. Sensory apparatus—sight, smell, taste, hearing, touch, coordination.
5. Energy levels—hyperactivity versus exhaustion, sleep, physical exercise.

6. Digestion/Assimilation—chronic upsets or deficiencies.
7. Eliminations—bowels, kidneys, liver, skin, lungs.
8. Muscular capability—tone, strength, endurance, coordination, relaxation, and elasticity.
9. Circulation—high/low blood pressure, heartbeat, endurance, edema, cold extremities, condition of blood and blood vessels.
10. Glandular balance—thyroid, adrenals, pituitary, sexual characteristics, etc.
11. Emotional responses—anger, fear, passive/aggressive, erotic, etc.
12. Cleanliness and care of teeth, skin, hair, lungs, liver, kidneys, bowels.
(You might try rearranging these twelve to fit your own order of their importance.)

Also, is there anything your body habitually craves which is essentially destructive or leads to withdrawal symptoms if you attempt to eliminate it? For example:

Cigarettes	Alcohol
Drugs	Sex
Certain foods	Beverages (coffee, tea, carbonated soda, etc.)

Again the reader may wish to add some item not listed, remembering that any negative habit, hangup, or imbalance is a stumbling block to spiritual growth. Yet with the proper attitude each can serve as a stepping-stone. Even Paul the apostle had his "thorn in the side." The following readings are indicative of this attitude.

We find from Mars that the entity has a very good temper; but *good* temper! One without a temper is in very bad shape, but one who can't control his temper is in still worse shape! (1857–2)

There is *power* even in anger. He that is angry and sinneth not controls self. He that is angry and allows such to become the expression in the belittling of self, or the self-indulgence of self in any direction, brings to self those things that partake of the spirit of that which is the product or influence of anger itself. (361-4)

From past incarnations—a high temper, yet one that will be very pleasant when everything is well; but a tendency to rule or ruin (others) is among the conditions of the entity to be overcome. (1346-1)

The entity is one to beware of in anger; one that often easily holds malice; one that holds grudges easily. Yet these very influences *spiritualized* may make for soul development, even though it passes through hardships, that will bring peace, happiness, joy, harmony. Are not these the opposite of hate, malice, and contention? (476-1)

A key to a change in attitude or acceptance of ills or imbalance can be found in this reading on "sacrifice."

Each should understand that *sacrifice does not necessarily mean a giving up, rather a glorifying for a definite purpose*—for an ideal, for a love . . . rather than a refraining from this or that. The choice must be made as to the purposefulness for which the activity is to be . . . and in keeping with what has been presented, that the bodies *are* the temples of the living God. (262-87)

For when duty, love and reason are one—then such consciousness approaches near that of Universal Love. (31)

BALANCED ACTIVITIES

Along with body balances—of physical/mental/emotional/spiritual—the reader should seriously consider his available time, effort, and direction within the framework of his daily life and overall life-style. It is fine to be outer directed in an effort to serve others, make a living, create a desirable home environment, keep abreast of the times, attend church or worship services, participate in hobbies, friendships, etc. But if these and other personal activities are not balanced values, then a certain amount of tension, conflict, and ambivalence will become apparent. Then too, there is the pitfall of becoming so busy and involved that we have no time for communing with self, or nature, or God—sometimes possibly as a ploy to avoid such spiritual confrontations. *Even Jesus had to withdraw himself from time to time for rest, prayer, and meditation. And today how few of us, weaker than He as we are, allow ourselves the same consideration?*

Too often we confuse work with progress and activity with accomplishment. Or, as Chaucer observed of an officious clerk, "Methinked he seemed busier than he was." So ask yourself, "Am I truly serving God by being overactive to the point of exhaustion while avoiding my spiritual exercises and needs?"

Many of us are prone to deceive ourselves by ignoring the significance of living in the present. The tremendous possibility of feasting upon each day as it comes, moment by moment, slips past us, and we are left searching for the rainbow, or dwelling in the past. Thomas Sugrue, Edgar Cayce's biographer and close friend, wrote of this in his hauntingly beautiful autobiographic novel, *Stranger in the Earth.*

But there is one danger which must not be overlooked. It is possible for the unit of perception to become snagged on a passing moment and dragged into the past, away from the eternal now. "Living in the past" is a common phrase for a common affliction. The function of evil is to tempt the soul to tarry in its journey, to entice it into inactivity; some of the webs of evil are spun of such subtle thread that only humor can detect them; morality stares at the trap and sees a clear passage.

No immorality is apparent, for instance, when an ego clings to the manners and fashions of a past era, the Victorian or Edwardian, for example. In fact it is common practice for persons jointly to endeavor to perpetuate and to extend to others the customs and habits of their group, piously pretending that these customs and habits comprise a moral code. Satire is the best defense against this particular device of Satan.

But the moment which snags the unit of perception need not be contained in the present lifetime of the ego. It may be a portion of the past, a part perhaps of the soul's pre-existence, if we wish to accommodate that theory. A man may be utterly immersed in a minor phase of Greek history, or the reign of a particular Ptolemy, or the French Revolution—

This holds true, as Sugrue observes and as we've mentioned before, in the business of dwelling upon past lives and karmic associations rather than "rising above it." Or, as that great old philosopher Satchel Paige has given us, "Don't look back—something might be gaining on you!"

For purpose of illustration, one way to consider a balance of activities is to diagram it thus:

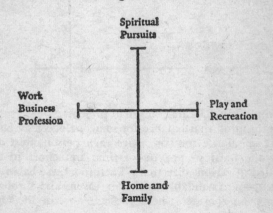

The typical hard-driving businessman might then be expressed as:

A playboy:

A housewife:

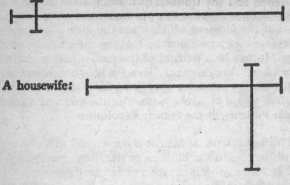

A minister:

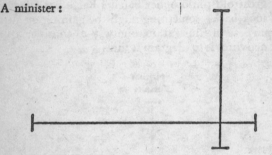

How would you diagram yourself at present?

Keep in mind that balance for someone else may be a decided imbalance for you, since each person must ascertain the ideal proportion of time and effort to be channeled in various directions. Then too, these balances will shift, understandably, with the seasons and through the years. So consider where you are now in life and judge accordingly.

And do find patience with self. It has been said, "Have we not piped all day and no one has answered?" Seekest thou, as given from this illustration, for the gratifying of thyself? Or seekest thou to be a channel of blessings to thy fellowman?

They may not have answered as *thou* hast seen. They may have even showed contempt or sneering for thy patience, and thy trouble. But *somewhere* the sun still shines—somewhere the day is done for those that have grown weary. For those that have given up—the *Lord abhorreth the quitter!* And those temptations that come in such cases are the viewing of thine own self. Ye have hurt thyself and ye have again crucified thy Lord when ye become impatient or speak harshly because someone has jeered or laughed at thy efforts. (518-2)

Finally, where would you place yourself at present in relation to these following extremes or opposites? And has this always been true for you?

Healthy	Unbalanced
Joyful	Envious
Happiness	Misery
Faith	Fear
Success	Failure
Growing	Depleting
Brotherhood	Prejudice
Masculine	Feminine
Freedom	Restrictions/Ties
Abundance	Poverty
Trust	Worry
Ability	Inferiority
Humility	Pride
Generosity	Greed
Elevating	Criticizing
Patience	Ill Temper
Peace	Tension/War
Strong	Weak
Flexible	Rigid
Giving/Sharing	Grasping
Forgiving	Resentful
Power-seeking	Loving
Indifferent	Selfless

Man's answer to everything has been *Power*—Power of money, Power of position, Power of wealth, Power of this, that, or the other. This has never been *God's* way, will never be God's way. (3976–9)

For God is love—and love is a "risk" decision.

For selfishness is the real sin, and as we become less and less conscious of self and more aware of being at an atonement with Him, greater may be the possibilities. (5625)

And, in our responsive positions we can only find a balance to God's love by ourselves being love. This is the symbology of the Cross and Crucifixion—for in Him we find the balance.

Chapter VIII

Changing Attitudes and Emotions

"Nothing in life is more certain than change—Still we resist change." Some years ago, before I ever heard of Edgar Cayce, I read an article on brain research that left an indelible impression. According to this article researchers were probing the exposed brain of a conscious individual, stimulating various nerve areas and observing the results. Finally, after a series of probes on the brain's motor areas which were causing movements in the patient's extremities, the patient observed, *"You're making me move my right arm."* Then came the eerie rejoinder: *"But you can't make me want to!"*

Where does the mind reside? The researchers as yet have not been able to pinpoint its location. The brain is centrally involved, to be sure, but no specific spot has been found that if stimulated will cause an individual to change his mind—or to make a decision—or specifically, to make him *want* to do something.

"So what do you want to do, Marty?"
"Gee, I don't know—What do you want to do?"

In my years as a classroom teacher and athletic coach I've often pondered the problems of motivation—how to get a child to *want* to learn about science, nature, his own body; how to impress an athlete with the fruits of desire, such things as excelling and winning. To be sure, a good teacher or coach can fire his students' enthusiasm, school spirit, and desire to participate, but in the final analysis, there is no way that a teacher, parent, or leader can effect a basic change in the attitudes and emotions of another individual other than by suggestion or personal example. Or, as someone has written, "What the children of the world need today are fewer critics and more good examples." The readings suggest that we should so live our lives that others will look to us and take it upon themselves to follow a similar pattern. This is what Jesus was demonstrating when He was able to say, "I am the Way."

We cannot change others, nor should we expect to. We can only change ourselves, and to do so we must "become as children." In the process we can influence others in a positive, creative fashion—which we may or may not have been doing in the past. Somewhat illustrative of this positive/negative influence we have on children is a tale from my own family closet of favorite stories. My mother's sister had two small youngsters who in their own home were continually being picked at and chewed out for this, that, and the other. At home they were generally uncontrollable for their parents, having to be disciplined and continually getting into everything. As the older child got to be five and six he was allowed to visit my parents' farm for days at a time. There he behaved perfectly well, cooperating in doing little chores, etc. No one had to ask him a second time to do or not to do anything. After his mother had observed this change of character a few times with some irritation, she finally cornered him and demanded, "Why don't you behave for me at home as you do at your Aunt B—'s?" The youngster looked her in the eye and shot back defiantly, "Well, 'cause *you make me like I am!*"

How many similar situations can we see as we look about us, in other people's lives, and in our own? The child was too young to realize why he was responding negatively or positively to his elders' dominant roles other than to blame the elders for his changes in behavior rather than himself. Still he himself was making the choice to change his behavior.

All of us have programmed ourselves similarly in this lifetime, from childhood on, and in other lifetimes as well. We behave one way with our peers, another way with family, still another way at work, etc. Again we should emphasize that no one, *but no one* other than self, *can change us or make us want to change!* That choice is the birthright of the soul—self's *free will*, coupled with desire.

BASIC CONCEPTS

A. *Only you can change self.* Others may aid, others impede, but only self, be free will, can change self. It is God's will and desire, and by His grace, that we have this opportunity to change for the better and return to atonement with Him.

Q: Should I pursue psychic development?
A: Pursue rather, spiritual development; this is of the psychic nature, yes, but find the spirit first—not spiritualism, but spirituality in thy own life. (3460–1)

That the entity comes seeking indicates it is of the house of Israel; and—seeking—there may indeed come that answer which will enable the entity to use this present experience as a stepping-stone for the unfoldment of a greater experience and walk with the consciousness of the spiritual life.

For, those that would seek knowledge and understanding seek same early—and when they are old they will not depart from that consciousness. (3272–1)

B. *Self-awareness in "knowing self" is fundamental to any change or desire for change.* As explained in previous chapters there must be some self-analysis and awareness of personal deficiencies or problems in addition to positive attributes. For, "The first step in the solution of a problem is to recognize the problem." Enlightenment and self-realization will follow as self accepts self. Along with this there must be a growing awareness of one's self-worth in relation to God.

C. *Any constructive change or desire for change must be founded upon one's ideals.*

In choosing then of self and self's activities, first know what is thy ideal—not merely as a theory but set it down on paper. Draw three lines and under each heading put: body; mind; material. God the Father; God the Son; God the Holy Spirit. Write the ideals in each under those headings also. Then find thy ideal under each. It will require time and patience and study of self, not judgments from others.

Ye are not a judge of thy fellowman. You can be a banker and tell him when he can borrow and when he can't, but don't become the judge!

And as ye judge (self) and as ye find in self, sincerity is the keynote of every individual soul. Who is sincere? One in a million! Ye can be one of those. Will ye? Try it!! (5249-1)

Q: What are my worst faults? Have I grown spiritually in this life?
A: These should be answered from looking into self. Who is to find fault with another? Look at thine own ideal, spiritually, mentally, materially, and compare thy real thoughts—not merely in mind, but write them down. You'll not be pleased with some, but it is the best way to make corrections—facing thine own self as in a mirror. (1298-3)

For the entity has rubbed out oft and begun all over again! And He loveth those who have repented. . . . This is not said of those who are hardheaded. (2390-1)

D. *There must be an attempt to answer the questions "Who am I and why am I here?"* Each of us must find or attempt to find the soul's purposes—reasons for which we came into the earth—in order to make our will the will of the Father. These purposes differ for each individual, and fortunately so—yet each of us must and should strive

to reach that state of consciousness where we can truly
state, "I and the Father are one!" (In purpose.)

Q: How may I know when the will to a course of action is justifiable, or when I am forcing my own personal will—which may lead to inaction, which is equally unjustifiable?
A: By the listening within—there is the answer. For, the answer to every problem, the answer to know His way, is ever within. . . . These appear at times to become contradictory, of course; but know—as the illustration has been used here—attunement, atonement, and at-onement are ONE; just as the inner is ever at work with the infinite within—for the lack of what would be called stamina, faith, patience, or whatnot. *Yet each entity, each soul, knows within when it is in an at-onement.* (2174–3)

As He hath given—"If ye abide with me, fear not as to problems, or even as to what ye shall answer; for in the selfsame hour it is given thee as to the choice to be made." (2403–1)
What is Love Divine? That the Father and the Son and the Holy Spirit may direct thee, does direct thee, *will* direct thee—in every thought, in every act. (262–104)

It is not that the Law alone is set and then the soul set adrift upon the sea of time or space, but *the* very abiding *presence* of the love of the Maker for the creature abides—if it (the individual) will but turn to same for its sorrows, its gladness, its hopes, its fears. For in Him is *love indeed,* and it casteth out fear. (920–1)

Q: What causes my inferiority complex?
A: It is NOT an inferiority complex; rather the lack of giving or allowing full expression of that INNATELY known to the entity from its deep experiences in matter, and the activities of the many.

Because of the FEAR of convention and what others will say.

Hence . . . ye may indeed learn the lesson as that Teacher of Teachers gave; that abiding in the truth, it SHALL make you free and (He) will bring to thy remembrance ALL that is helpful since the foundations of that ye know as the earth. (1473-1)

E. *Finally, you have to want to change!* There must be a sincere desire and reason for wanting to effect change and a strong willingness to see it through!

You are working under conditions that to you are not satisfactory—if you had the ideal conditions you wouldn't give your best either! And don't fool yourself that you would! Because he that says he would give to the poor if he had a million, and doesn't give when he has ten cents, wouldn't give if he had a million! The same applies in the preparations of those things that represent ideals and principles and purposes. Not that ye are perfect but that ye would *grow.* (1800-28)

DECISIONS DECISIONS

Prior to any discussion of techniques used in effecting change there must be a decision *to* change. For wanting to change or desiring to change merely supplies power for the potential movement of the spirit or psyche. Only a clear-cut decision will allow the spirit to move as it should. And since most of us have made so many poor decisions and movements in the past we are often inclined toward indecision or lack of direction.

Q: Is what is holding me back physical or laziness?
A: Rather that of indecision, incontriteness. Purge thy mind, thy body. Make thyself one with Him.

Q: Why do I not make a more continuous effort?
A: Is thy purpose a single one? or art thou seeking— seeking without putting into practice that thou knowest? (922-1)

Q: How have I failed to use wisely what God has given me? Why am I so confused about so many things?

A: Do not—do not feel that ye have failed. Do not judge self. *You have not failed YET! You only fail if you quit trying.* The trying is oft counted for righteousness. Remember as He has given, "I do not condemn thee! Go, be patient, be kind, and the Lord be with thee!" (3297–1)

It is the "try" that is the more often counted as righteousness, and not the success or failure. Failure to anyone should be a stepping-stone and not a millstone. (931–1)

The decision then should be *"I'll try,"* or *"I'll try one more time."* Best not to make vows and promises to self or others. For example, have you ever promised or sworn to keep a secret? And did you? The Bible admonishes us not to swear oaths, "But let thy yeas be yea, and thy nays be nay."

Very probably the depth of one's commitment to a decision for change will be directly tied to an emotional experience. IT IS NOT ENOUGH SIMPLY TO INTELLECTUALIZE ONE'S DESIRES FOR CHANGE, for unless one's willpower and self-discipline are exceedingly strong and controlled the decisions more than likely will soon be forgotten and laid aside. Ideally, for one to change he should first experience a profound emotional or psychic, mystical experience—akin to Paul on the road to Damascus. Since most of us are not usually blessed with such memorable initial confrontations with the spirit, we shall touch upon a variety of techniques that have been used successfully in producing effective decision-making and follow-through.

In considering decisions we might well compare our spiritual sluggishness to the mule in that memorable tale —being struck vigorously and methodically over the head by a professed mule trainer. When the mule's owner declared he wanted him trained, not killed, the trainer declared, "Oh, I'll start larnin' him real soon, but first I got to get the so-and-so's attention!"

FAITH—ACCEPTANCE

Assuming that we now have the attention of our psyche and a decision has been made to move in a specific direction, then we must surround that decision with an air of faith, trust, and acceptance. If as individuals we can move in life with the inner courage of conviction and awareness of consequence that Jesus had after his decision to go into Jerusalem, then we too may attain that attunement of knowing our will is the will of the Father—knowing that, in purpose, "I and the Father are one."

Where we fail generally is in keeping to our decisions and fully accepting the consequences of our acts over extended periods of time. All too often we want instant results, overnight cures for the ills of a lifetime—"Spiritual perfection within seven days or our money back." The readings state that there are no shortcuts to God. To my way of thinking (and this is supported by the readings) the individual who receives a "baptism of the Holy Spirit" or testifies a decision to "accept Christ" has very probably had that emotional experience necessary to effect change—*as a commencement award or graduation exercise, not as an end-all*—and henceforth lies the opportunity to apply the fruits of the spirit in everyday living. Jesus, for example, did not stop working for humanity after His baptism or His resurrection. In modern parlance He "had it made," but He still continues His work in the earth (I believe) as part of a deep personal commitment—and will continue to do so for as long as one lost soul remains. For modern man to refrain from joining this effort on the presumption of already "being saved" is an error in this writer's opinion.

Another level of faith and acceptance is in the physical circumstances surrounding our individual existences. Nature, chance, human happenings, comings and goings all play a part in what at times may appear to us as a bewildering hodgepodge of events. But the readings state that "nothing happens by chance." The readings observe that "accidents can happen." However, in the long run,

ye will find, as has been the injunction from the beginning, be ye of one mind. (2995–3)

As we find, then, we would give that first, in making for corrections, there must be a change of attitude—towards self, those about self, and the conditions which the body physically and mentally has found and does find around self. Resentments, animosities, petty jealousies, and the like must be eliminated as much as practical and possible, IF there will be the better physical force, the better mental and physical reaction. (1889–1)

BE A JOYOUS RECEIVER

Accept *being* a joyous receiver of God's gifts *and* the gifts of others. We've often heard that refrain, "The Lord loves a cheerful giver!" But how often have we applied the reverse of being glad receivers?

All too frequently there is that unfortunate rejoinder, of "Oh, you *shouldn't* have," whenever someone does something for us, or presents us with a gift. "Oh, you shouldn't have" is really a "put-down" in a sense—because *of course they should have! It* is not for us to question a gift or the intent of the giver of gifts—especially those the Lord sends our way.

So be a joyous receiver and you'll make the giving of gifts a joy to the giver—particularly to the Giver of all gifts.

(Tolkien's Hobbits are a delightful and refreshing example of the spirit of receiving and giving.)

BEGIN WITH THE BODY

Then sing a lot about the work—in everything the body does. Hum, sing—to self; *not to be heard by others* but be heard by self. (3386–1)

Then see the joy, even in sorrow. See the pleasures that may even come with pain. (3440–2)

The keynote to preparing the body for changes, both physical and mental, is found in that fascinating word "discipline." The followers of the Master were not called "disciples" by chance. There were disciplines to be accepted, shared, and put into practice. So how shall we regard self-discipline in defining and understanding it? By my definition, DISCIPLINE IS THE WILLINGNESS TO ACT AND APPLY IN A PURPOSEFUL MANNER—IN ACCORD WITH WHAT HAS BEEN ACCEPTED AS THE IDEAL.

There is, to be sure, a difference between *being* disciplined by others and disciplining self. And while we are concerning ourselves here with the latter, in one very real sense we are always *being* disciplined by the higher self, or Christ-consciousness. Again the conscious self's responsive role holds the key to our inner relationship with that dominant aspect of self. *Thus our spiritual retardation varies in direct proportion with our unwillingness to discipline self toward inner balance and attunement.*

THE FIRST STEP IN PREPARATION FOR DISCIPLINES IS TO MAKE AN AFFIRMATION. Affirmations as given in the readings are closely akin to prayers, with special emphasis on the personal will's being involved—as with "I will" in the following. (This affirmation is one we use regularly and recommend for others as well.) "FATHER GOD—*I WILL* THAT THIS ACTIVITY CREATES IN ME A GREATER CHANNEL *THAT THY WILL BE DONE.*"

There are various traditional disciplines which may be considered. These are a matter of personal preference, dependent primarily on the individual's most immediate needs and objectives. The first group are those in the category, "This would be well for all."

1. Prayer and Meditation (humbling self).
2. Diet and exercise.
3. Dream-recording and analysis.
4. Bible study, group study.
5. Being of service to others (again humbling self)—social work, community projects, etc.

Other worthwhile possibilities can be found in:

6. Periods of fasting and maintaining silence.
7. Singing and chanting.
8. Breathing and relaxation techniques.
9. Various related yoga disciplines and exercises.
10. Mental control—memory, positive thinking, healing, etc.

The specific techniques involved in any of the above-mentioned disciplines are too complicated and lengthy for inclusion here. Each deserves volumes in itself and indeed many books have been compiled concerning most. For further study we suggest the ARE study group program and publications list as a basic reference.

Finally, in any and all disciplines we suggest that beyond the basic affirmation the following be incorporated as a continual refrain and reaffirmation.

SEVEN CARDINAL VIRTUES IN ATTAINING SELF-DISCIPLINE

1. Dedication (A decision)
2. Motivation (A commitment)
3. Willpower (The desire)
4. Persistence (The application)
5. Consistence (Being steady, habitual)
6. Patience (Attaining acceptance)
7. Expectancy (Maintaining faith)

Then through trials, troubles, tribulations, one arrives at the best things in life, and the trials are forgotten. (288–1)

BEGIN A NEW LIFE

There is much to be said in favor of having an individual spiritual rebirth, with its accompanying emotional impact: *"Ye must be reborn, to enter the kingdom of heaven."* As previously suggested this may or may not happen spontaneously. It may come in spurts—bits and pieces of spiritual awakenings over extended periods of time. There are ways, however, of quickening these changes and awakenings, concurrent with maintaining the necessary physical and mental disciplines. Again we should stress *balance* because if the foundations underlying future changes have not been properly laid in accord with the concepts given in these chapters, then the individual seeker may simply go on and on in self-delusion, or worse.

Fundamental to this is the psychological fact that any attempt to suppress destructive personal habit patterns is futile in the long run, and the readings confirm this. All forms of repression, substitution, or rationalization are equally ineffective, too. Indeed, there is much to support the observation that the more times we attempt to suppress a bad habit without success—heavy cigarette addiction, drug addiction, compulsive eating or drinking —the stronger its hold on us becomes when it again takes over. The epic struggles between Hercules and Atlas seem to parallel this. Each time Hercules fought Atlas and threw him to the ground, the vengeful Atlas arose growing stronger than before, until Hercules knew that if Atlas came back one last time he would be overpowered.

In similar fashion destructive thought patterns may lie submerged in our unconscious karmic bodies much like electronic "memory loops" waiting to be replayed on demand by our selfish or violent desires. Then the more we toy with them or eventually struggle to suppress them and put them down, the stronger their imprint becomes, until the individual borders on emotional imbalance, obsession, or other mental instabilities.

Hercules won over Atlas by ceasing the attempts to destroy his antagonist by combat. Hercules found that if he raised Atlas overhead, Atlas was weakened. In the same way we should raise our consciousness of our self-destructive tendencies through prayer and meditation, through love and service—and in effect, dissolve them. Both the Eastern philosophies and the Cayce readings point to this as the only truly successful way to overcome destructive habit patterns—by eliminating desires, through detachment and growing above and beyond them: "If thy right hand offend thee, cut it off!" Similarly, if a thought pattern offends thee, cut it off. But don't fight it—dissolve it—as if it never was. There is considerable personal testimony to support the theory that what prayer and meditation actually accomplish in the body is a washing away, or erasing, of the negative/destructive memory imprints submerged in our unconscious. So when the Easterners attest that "Fifteen minutes of meditation each day can wash away the sins of a thousand lifetimes," they are attesting to actual physical changes.

RITUAL AND COVENANTING

The traditional methods of signifying rebirth, growth, and transformation are found in all cultures and religions. These are still extremely valid today in our personal experience if we can but contact the truth behind our age-old symbols of ritual, initiation, celebration of sacraments, and holy days—the breaking of bread and sharing of wine—especially the significance of "covenanting."

Theologians have long pointed to seven covenants, the last given by the Master to His disciples—the first to Adam—as contacts between God and Man, with varying rules or contracts being laid before us in the process. These covenants have often been looked upon as a necessity because of man's failure in the earth. But the Cayce materials take a more positive view, pointing to them as an upward-evolving set of standards for an evolving body of mankind. The last of the commandments, "the New Covenant" as given by the Master, is probably the least understood of all. Any reasonably fair observation of so-called Christian nations, societies, or institutions over the past two thousand years must conclude with general agreement that His command that "Ye must love one another" has survived as a rather hollow phrase with little application in the affairs of men or nations.

Yet each day, as individuals, we have the opportunity of reaffirming His covenant with us—in prayer and meditation, in our comings and goings, in dealing with our fellowmen. So consider this covenanting as a necessary step in spiritual transformation that goes hand in hand with mental/emotional changes. Also, if it is your custom to do so, partake of the rituals, sacraments, and celebrations of your own religion in the fullest sense of awareness regarding their significance.

From an individual standpoint, beginning a new life may be found in a change of scenery—a vacation, a retreat, or a physical move, new friends or different work, even a change of name (Simon to Peter, as an illustration). Here though, we must consider our motives and seriously question such changes on the basis of whether they are made as an escape from personal problems or responsibilities, or whether some thing or some relationship is being left behind that has served only to drag one down or thwart one's purpose in life. Apropos of such, what if Jesus had said to himself, "No, Mother is a widow and needs me, I can't hurt her by leaving now. And it would be far more than she could bear if I ended up being crucified!"

As with Him, each of us must find our own soul purposes and live by them. As we find in *Hamlet*, "This above all: to thine own self be true."

RELATING TO OTHERS

Most of us are in need of reeducating ourselves in relation to our attitudes about others and how we think about them. The philosopher Martin Buber has expressed one phase of this very eloquently in his concepts of "I—Thou" relationships* rather than "I—You" or "I—It." Thus if we regard others as simply "you" or as objects (or "its") rather than seeing the God force being expressed through them, we are treating them again as less than human and the relationship suffers. Basic to any

* *I and Thou*, by Martin Buber.

change in attitudes toward others is maintaining a consciousness of this "I—Thou" relationship.

Put self in other's situations. It has also been well stated that no man would criticize another if he first walked a mile in the other man's shoes. How often are we inclined to prejudge or condemn the actions or motives of others? The readings suggest we take that burden of responsibility off our own shoulders and leave it to the Lord! For, "As ye judge so are ye judged."

If you can truly empathize with others—with all their faults, failures, and and inadequacies—the indication is that you may never have to face such conditions in your own life. The examples of "Boomerang Karma" within the readings show over and over again that the very things some individuals condemned in previous lives had now come back to haunt them. Thus, "As you condemn so are ye condemned—as ye forgive so may ye be forgiven."

Self-pride and self-pity should be considered, too, in regard to others. I've always reminded my students of that old aphorism that no matter how big and strong or tough and smart you are, and set out to prove it, sooner or late there will come a time when you'll meet another person just a little bit bigger and stronger or tougher and smarter! This holds true on the other end of the scale too, for no matter how badly off a person can be, he can invariably find someone in worse condition than himself. (From an old Indian proverb: "I cried for I had no shoes. Then I met a man who had no feet.")

SEEING OURSELVES AS OTHERS SEE US

(Don't attempt too much of this until you've developed humor, humility, and a strong appreciation for the absurd—otherwise it hurts too much.—J.F.)

Some very effective techniques have been developed and employed in this area through the use of psychodrama and various types of "group grope" or encounter groups. (Alcoholics Anonymous would serve as one ideal type of the latter, plus Esalen, or the ARE "Search for God" study groups.)

There can be some personal trauma, however, in entering group-encounters or psychodrama situations if they are not founded on ethical behavior or based on a stated ideal of being helpful and healing in the awareness of all concerned. Otherwise, an encounter situation can be very explosive to the personality structure of a basically unbalanced individual. In addition many of the encounter situations afford an ideal situation for those who enjoy "playing games" with people—for whatever motives. (Power, sex, money, or "using others" are among the primary games.) Unless one is pretty well-balanced, can be very honest with himself, and has trust in whoever is controlling the encounter situations, our advice would be to seek safer channels for self-awareness.

Historically, the first well-documented encounter group is found in the New Testament—Peter, James, John, and the rest. Unfortunately not all of our groups today have the benefits of such a talented Leader.

OTHER QUESTIONABLE OR PROBLEMATIC TECHNIQUES

In addition to questionably idealized sensitivity or encounter group situations, there are a number of other areas which should be approached with caution or studiously avoided. Not that some of these cannot bring about constructive awarenesses and effect changes, it's just that a great number of present-day psychological "basket cases" bear out the risks involved. These include: psychedelic drugs, witchcraft and occult practices, ouija boards and table tipping, automatic writing, astral projection, mediumship and attempts to contact the dead, giving psychic readings, prophesying, fortune-telling, hypnosis and autosuggestion, extreme Yoga disciplines without proper preparation, and faith healing (in lieu of medical consultation). *Dianetics, Scientology, and Mind Control groups can also effect dramatic changes, but again, as with encounter groups, the leadership and motives can be problematical.*

COMMUNAL LIVING

As an ideal situation communal living offers a tremendous opportunity for an individual to experience personal growth in the areas of cooperation, sharing, creativity, communication, self-reliance, and integrity. If the communal group is self-sustaining, producing its own food in natural surroundings, the contacts with nature can be especially beneficial for a previous city dweller. And if a group is strongly dedicated to spiritual advancement, the changes in basic attitudes and emotions can be quite dramatic.

Unfortunately, not all communal setups are ideal. As many former "dropouts" have observed after years in numerous communes, the phonies and deadbeats, the con artists and hustlers are all there too—just like in straight society—only the uniforms and language have been changed to conform with another life-style.

As a supplement to this chapter we suggest that the reader study *Forms and Techniques of Altruistic and Spiritual Growth*—A Symposium Edited by Pitirim Sorokin, Beacon Press, 1954. This book contains a comprehensive evaluation of Zen and yoga disciplines, the Psychodrama Technique of J. L. Moreno, studies on prayer, mechanisms for change by F. M. Alexander, and methods of education in Mennonite and Hutterite communities. Of the latter communal groups it is stated (p. 295):

True education is fundamentally a matter of practical example—*Nobody is able to educate others,* whether adults, young people, or children, so as to arouse in them a creative and altruistic attitude toward their fellow men, *unless he himself is motivated by the power of love in all his conscious or unconscious acts and behavior.* The basic personal attitude necessary for the success of integral community life is of a twofold nature, and can best be described as an attitude of *responsibility* and *humility*. (Italics mine.)

We are responsible for one another and for all aspects of the life of the group of which we are an integral part. This responsibility can only be exercised, however, if the spirit of true humility is present at the same time. Pride, ambition, the will to push oneself forward, as well as the overestimation of one's own value, are disruptive and divisive forces which lead to strife and conflict within a group; unless these destructive impulses and their resulting actions are curbed, they will eventually lead to the dissolution and disintegration of community. (Again the dominant/responsive role problem!)

How, then, can these two cardinal virtues, responsibility and humility, be acquired? *First of all, there must be a religious experience, truly personal in character, but universal and all-comprehensive in its meaning and scope.* The individual must come to a realization of his own failure to live in harmony with the laws of love and unity.

The commentary goes on to provide a mechanism for change:

It still seems to be one of the hardest tasks in the world, to persuade an individual to sift his hostile attitudes and to separate correctly the causes that lie "out there" from the causes that lie "in here."

Awareness without control, however, is of no practical value, and to make a man aware of the desirability of change without giving him the ability to make it (himself) is to do him a disfavor.

The Socratic precept that "knowledge is virtue" has meaning only if knowledge broadens its scope to include knowledge of how to change. (Or, as the Cayce materials note: "Knowledge not applied is sin." Better never to have known!)

The F. M. Alexander technique as detailed in the So-rokin *Symposium* is another consideration. (The author has added to this from his own experience and usage.) This is a method employed to bring about psychophysical changes, or "reprogramming" by teaching the individual to recognize and prevent habitual automatic reactions and responses that interfere with rational thought processes and decision-making choices. We might consider this technique as "nonreaction," "counting to ten," or even "keeping one's cool." It involves: 1) control (non-reaction) of any initial automatic response to a situation, command, or immediate desire; 2) an awareness of the immediate stress patterns—physical/mental/emotional potentials—aroused by the nonreaction (Alexander also notes various body posture orientations. We might also ask ourselves, "Why?" as to the reactions; 3) a sense of detachment, moving to the inner affirmation of "Thy will be done," followed by; 4) a guided (responsive) decision to act or not to act. This self-imposed decision may be further checked by 5) asking the inner consciousness "yes or no?" If yes, continue. If no, reconsider! This is very effective for the author, as a lecturer, during question-and-answer periods—where a harsh or poorly thought-out answer could well lead to misunderstandings.

An excellent starting point for using the above method is in regard to our own temper. For as the readings have observed:

Remember, no man is bigger than that which makes him lose his temper. (255–55)

He that is able to control his own temper his own purposes, is greater than he that may even take seven cities. (1610–2)

Finally, effecting change within by taking on disciplines is usually more difficult when it's done alone. Having a partner or a group with similar objectives can spell the difference between success or failure in staying with the disciplines over an extended period of time. Among the varied branches of Eastern thought some believe that a "teacher" or "guru" is necessary for ultimate advancement. This may be true for some individuals, but such a personal master should never supplant *the* Master and Teacher of teachers in our opinion.

How long should our disciplines be maintained? The following reading gives us a clue in regard to a seven-year cycle:

In the body we find that which connects the pineal, the pituitary, the lyden, may truly be called the silver cord, or the golden cup that may be filled with a closer walk with that which is the creative essence in physical, mental, and spiritual life; for the destruction wholly of either (of the three centers) will make for the disintegration of the soul from its house of clay.

To be purely material minded, were an anatomical or pathological study made for a period of seven years (which is a cycle of change in all the body elements) of one that is acted upon through the third eye alone, we will find one fed upon spiritual things becomes a light that may shine from and in the darkest corner. One fed upon the purely material will become a Frankenstein (monster) that is without a concept of any influence other than material or mental. (262–20)

Why not try it for seven years and see what happens?

Chapter IX

Health and Healing

There are in truth no incurable conditions, for the condition is the breaking of a law, and the healing forces will of necessity become the compliance with other laws that meet the needs of the condition. *The healing depends upon the individual, and the attitude taken toward conditions.* (3744–1)

Know that there is within self all healing that may be accomplished for the body. For all healing must come from the Divine! For who healeth thy diseases?—the source of the universal supply! *As the attitude, then, of self, how well do ye wish to be?* How well are ye willing to cooperate, coordinate with the divine influences which may work in and through thee, by stimulating the centers which have been latent with nature's activities. For all of these forces must come from the One Source—and the applications (or treatments) are merely to stimulate the atoms of the body. For each cell is as a representative of a universe in itself. Then what would ye do with thy abilities? As ye give to others, not hating them (but aiding them), to know more of the Universal Forces—so may ye have the more, for God is love. (4021–1)

For the body renews itself, every atom, in seven years. How have ye lived for the last seven? And then the seven before? *What would ye do with thy mind and thy body if they were wholly restored to normalcy in this experience?* Would these be put to the use of gratifying thine own appetites as at first? Will these be used for the magnifying of the appreciation of the love to the infinite? For who healeth all thy diseases? If ye think it is the doctor or the surgeon, who is thy doctor? Is his life different from your own? *Life itself, comes from the Infinite. There ye must begin . . .* if ye would have healing for this body. (3684-1)

Q: Are the nerves of motivation dead?
A: If they are, may they not be renewed? Isn't the body renewed at least once every seven years? Who is to renew it? Who is the giver of life? By pure coordination, pure faith, pure desire to be what God would have thee be. (5326-1)

(For a woman with multiple sclerosis.)

Remember, the source of this condition is the meeting of yourself: it is karmic. This can be met best in Him who, taking away the law of cause and effect by fulfilling the law, *established the Law of Grace.* Thus the need for the entity to lean on the arm of Him who is the Law, and the Truth, and the Light.

As we find, there are disturbances and these are all the progressive type of a form of multiple sclerosis, that will gradually cause more anxiety and more and more pain—unless there is that hope or belief attained within self's consciousness that there may be administrations made which have helped others and which will help the body.

There must first be, then, that correct attitude toward the Creative Energies, call it Spiritualism, Divine Science, God, Christ, or whatever name. Know that self can be, and is by heritage, a part of that First Cause. (5129-1)

If Edgar Cayce had ever been approached by medical examiners to determine his own medical specialty, the final conclusion would have to have been, as the readings show, that Cayce specialized in man's entirety—the whole man—with an interinvolvement of all ramifications of man's past/present/future—body/mind/spirit. Invariably in the readings there was the refrain of spiritual awareness tied to the whole of creation. Each individual disease or condition was considered by Cayce along the lines of the basic precepts discussed in earlier chapters. *All* illness, indeed the *only* cause of illness *was self*, which in turn was equated with sin, or self's error from the path of spiritual at-onement with God.

At first this may seem an oversimplification, especially when we consider various bewilderingly complex diseases. But when we view the basic complexity of human life through all stages of our development—conception, birth, childhood, puberty, adulthood, through till dissolution—it is amazing that most bodies maintain the balance and vitality of life forces that they do. An interesting observation can be made in regard to several problematical, pathological conditions the causes of which psychiatrists have found perplexing, and which are generally regarded as incurable. They can be treated, with varying degrees of success, to suppress symptoms, yet the basic conscious/unconscious personality drives still persist. They include schizophrenia, heroin addictions, alcoholism, homosexuality and hardened, amoral criminal types. In each case, the only individuals who have broken the pattern and been truly healed—as with a former alcoholic who can now take an occasional drink with no compulsion to continue—are those who somewhere along the line have had a deep, stirring religious/mystical confrontation that completely changes their lives. Certain types of mental phobias and compulsions (such as gambling) also seem to relate in much the same manner.

OUR IMMEDIATE PREMISE IS THAT ALONG WITH BASIC CHANGES IN ATTITUDES AND EMOTIONS, PERMANENT HEALING CANNOT BE EFFECTED WITHOUT A DEEP PERSONAL CONFRONTATION WITH SELF, AKIN TO WHAT HAS BEEN DESCRIBED AS A RELIGIOUS/MYSTICAL EXPERIENCE. Short of that we are merely patching up the cracks in our psyches rather than rebuilding the foundations. We can dry out an alcoholic, imprison a violent criminal or drug addict, institutionalize the schizophrenics, but where have we progressed so far as actual health and healing are concerned? True, symptoms need to be treated, and rightfully so, but it is time that we faced up to the essential spiritual causality of healing and disease. For many of us perhaps our final healing will only be accomplished in the hereafter, assuming we've lived up to our soul purposes during this lifetime. Meanwhile, there are many factors in health and healing to be considered while we are in the earth.

As noted previously, we are currently building the basis for the child we will be the next time around. For the readings indicate that the finer (physical or astral) body goes with us into death as a potential, and emerges in the next life with many of the same strengths and weaknesses that have been built into it. So just because one reaches an advanced age doesn't mean that he should begin letting things slide by or giving up! We have touched upon some facets of this in our book *The Return of Frances Willard*. Therein a Cayce reading given for a fifteen-day-old girl in 1939 identified the child as having been Frances Willard, the famed nineteenth-century Temperance leader. The physical resemblance of "Stephanie" at present compared to Frances Willard at the same age is quite remarkable. Additionally, some of Frances' physical and mental attributes seem to have carried over: weak lungs, strong temper, and a preference for certain types of furniture and household items are just a smattering of the similarities we've found—along with a strong devotion to Christ in both lives.

For the soul seeks its own—in Him who is the Light, the Life, the Way, and when there are rebellions of body or mind against this search—is there any wonder that atoms of the body cause high blood pressure, indigestion, etc.? For all such reactions are only the rebellion against Truth and Light, error and correction in a physical body—and thy body is indeed the temple of the Living God.

What have ye dragged into this Temple? (3174-1)

The following readings and commentary on multiple sclerosis have been extracted from an ARE *Searchlight* article, "The Power of Attitudes in Serious Diseases" by Gladys Davis Turner.

These extracts give only a small portion of the overall etiology that the readings ascribed to multiple sclerosis. Lengthy prescribed treatments have been excluded so that we may focus primarily on the emphasis given to the attitudes in each case.

MULTIPLE SCLEROSIS

(A general reading on the disease itself, requested by a doctor.)

Mrs. C.: You will have before you the request of Charles G. Taylor, M.D., for a research reading on the disease known as multiple sclerosis. You will consider the following statement from Dr. Taylor: "The material pathology: multiple sclerosis is a disease of nerve fibers in the spinal cord and brain. The insulating sheaths of these fibers are evidently attacked by some destructive agent which causes them to melt away and be replaced by fibrous tisue." Please answer the following questions:

Mr. C.: In giving the true pathological condition, as we find, this condition of the spinal cord and of the brain is rather the *result of conditions* arising in the assimilative system, from a *lack of balance* in the hormones of the blood supply. And it is then a nerve condition; but (one of nerves) impoverished from a lack of this condition (hormone) in the blood stream—or in the glandular forces which supply, from the system, those elements necessary to give an elasticity or the activity which is necessary.

The condition, of course, may be said to be a law unto itself, in each individual. This, to be sure, is dependent upon that very influence from which the activity of the first cell is taken, in a body or entity.

Now, just as the nerve system is that channel through which the atomic energies—or electronic atomic energies—pass to become active; so there is, then, the lack of certain elements within the system; and (the lack) in the body's abilities to produce that of gold through its activity in the assimilative system.

The history of the case itself must be considered; and the effect there has been upon the parentage, as to a sufficient amount of the cellular force around each of these atomic forces that go to make up the first cell, or the fetus itself. Then it is the effect of gold, the atomic effect of gold, that should be added to the system.

The reproductive glands first become noticed, as to their lack of those elements for reproduction. Then when this is discovered—the lack in these—then there should be the addition of the gold necessary.

This is presupposing that it (gold, vibratorily) is taken with the first symptoms, see? Or with the beginning of sterility or such inactivity from the system, as it may be called. (907)

THE GLANDS

Notice the above references to the glands and the first activity about the cell and then consider this extract from a general reading on the endocrine system.

. . . this is the system whereby, or in which, the dispositions, characters, natures, and races all have their source. . . . There is an activity within the system produced by anger, fear, mirth, joy, or any of those activities which flow into the whole of the system.

There is, then, in the system, that activity of the soul which is the gift of the Creator to man. It may be easily seen, then, how very closely the glands are associated with reproduction, degeneration, and regeneration; and this not only throughout the physical forces of the body but throughout the mental body and the soul body. The *glandular forces, then, are ever akin to the sources from which—through which—the soul dwells within the body.*

That is, *what effect does it have upon you even to get mad, to laugh, to cry, to be sorrowful? All of these activities affect not only yourself and your relationships to your fellowman, but also your next experience in the earth!* (281–38)

SPECIFIC CASES, SPECIFIC ATTITUDES

Extracts from readings on multiple sclerosis: Case 3114, female, seventeen, multiple sclerosis for ten years.

If it will be accepted, this is a purging of the body; thus a prenatal condition, or a choice by the entity to enter this particular environ. Yet those making administrations to give help for this body may change the whole course of this entity's unfoldment.

First there is a need, we find, to get the cooperation of the body itself, so that those impressions may be made upon creative influences in the body. *This will require a spiritual awakening and a mental alertness* . . . the body has grown so "don't-care" in some respects that this will require some effort on the part of those responsible for the body.

Case 4005, male, thirty-eight. Sister requested reading; no history submitted.

As we find, there are disturbances that are both pathological and psychological in nature . . . or, those that are Karmic. *If there is a change in the body's attitude, there may be some counteraction to the general weakening forces . . .* the present deterioration of the abilities of activities in the locomotories.

Then do not become "self-pitying or egotistical," or . . . condemning others for their attitude or their lack of consideration. First, then, add to the body brotherly love, patience and consistency. Whatever the disturbance, do not lose a sense of humor, but be patient. Do show brotherly love and kindness.

Case 5129, female, forty-nine, multiple sclerosis, also arthritis.

Q: Can a permanent cure be obtained?
A: This depends upon the consistency, *and the general mental and spiritual attitude of the entity.*
Q: Should all present treatments be discontinued?
A: This depends . . . on the body finding in self that which will answer for . . . *ideals in the spiritual and mental attitudes of the entity.*
Q: What mental assistance can the body render herself?
A: *Read what has been given.* This (help) must be by that which the entity holds as the source of its own divine nature.

KARMA AND FORGIVENESS

Case 2828, male, forty, spinal deterioration:

. . . *the entity is meeting self. . . . When it was given,* "Whosoever sheddeth man's blood, by man shall his blood be shed," *that (means) in this case the blood of his will, of his purpose, of his physical desire to carry on in his own ways of activity . . . and, by these conditions in the body itself, being thwarted. The entity thwarted others, and is meeting it in self. That is karma.*

In the blood of the Christ which was shed, karma is met and then it becomes the law—not of cause and effect but of being justified by faith in Him. Then we may use, and we may apply, things of the material earth and in spiritual combination to become again sons of God.

Q: Approximately how long will it be before I will improve?

A: How long before tomorrow, Mr. A.? How long is the power of God in self? *How long does it take thee to do His biddings? How long hast thou kept in the way beyond reproach of thine own self, as well as in the way of being a helpful influence in the experience of each one ye meet day by day?*

Case 5268, male, thirty-two, multiple sclerosis for ten years. No hope offered by doctors; mother requested reading:

Yes, we have the physical being and body. . . . We have here an entity meeting its own self. The gentler, the kinder others may be to this body, the greater the help that may come to the soul-entity, to learn patience, to learn tolerance in the physical—to obtain coordination of the mind, or mental with physical. Deterioration is too far advanced for individual help, other than (what) may be administered to the body for its soul development.

There may be only a few years, but don't make them harder. Do be gentle. This will make the time longer, but do be patient, do show brotherly love. For as ye would be forgiven, forgive. As ye would be loved, love. As ye would have kindness shown, show kindness and gentleness. For this is the work of the Lord.

The above is the complete reading for Case 5268, which was given in June of 1944. In October, the subject's mother wrote, in answer to a questionnaire:

. . . I awaited the reading for my son with increased interest. Several friends with interests along these lines feel it completely answered our questions regarding my son, "an entity meeting its own self." My son is still alive, bed-ridden for many years; and I have been working for the MS Society, trying to interest sufferers to band together and make their cases available for research and medical study. *I find so many of them with this type of personality that I cannot help wondering if the cause of the ailment is not in the personality,* rather than of physical or medical unbalance. . . . We have tried to follow EC's advice to be gentle and patient and show brotherly love—and it has indeed made the time longer. . . . The doctors do not know how he keeps alive.

In 1949 the mother wrote: "My son died February 2. I found the reading of great interest because my son seemed for so long to be *a dual personality, warring against itself,* thus destroying himself physically. Since his death, I have observed that many people with MS have somewhat the same personalities."

Another interesting reading on multiple sclerosis was that given for Case 3124, male of thirty-four, unable to work for three years, charity case; nurse at a charity farm requested the reading:

As is understood by some and thought by many: within each physical being there exist the elements whereby the organs and their activities and functionings are enabled, within themselves, to supply what is needed for replenishing or rebuilding their own selves. This may be done, as comprehended, within a period of every seven years. Thus it is a slow process; but it is a growth in the energies of the body. . . . We find what is commonly called the law of cause and effect, or karmic conditions, being met by an individual entity. For as given of old, each soul shall give an account of every idle word spoken. It shall pay every whit!

The entity, then, is still at war with itself. But all hate, all malice, all that would make man afraid must first be eliminated from the mind of the individual entity.

Six months later, another reading for this same case stated:

As we find, there have been physical improvements in the body—yet much, much is to be desired. As indicated . . . *this is a karmic condition and there must be measures taken for the body to change its attitude toward conditions, things, and its fellowman.*

As long as there were practical applications of mechanical things for physical correction—and concerted efforts by the body's friends to make intercession in prayer—improvements were indicated. *When the body becomes so self-satisfied, so self-centered as to . . . refuse or does not change its attitude;* as long as there are hate, malice, injustice . . . jealousy . . . that which is at variance to patience, long-suffering, brotherly love, kindness, and gentleness—*there cannot be healing* for that condition of this body. . . . But first, the change of heart, the change of mind, the change of intent.

Thy body is indeed the temple of the living God. And how does it appear in the present? Broken in purpose; broken in the ability to reproduce itself!

And what is lacking? That which is life itself: which is of—and manifestation of—that influence or force ye call God, God in manifestation. Will ye accept or will ye reject? It is up to thee. We are through, unless ye make amends. (3124)

Gladys Davis Turner concludes her *Searchlight* commentary with these well-chosen views:

In summary, it would seem that multiple sclerosis victims are at war within themselves, and the body is the battleground. The enemy would seem to be hate, malice, condemnation of self and others, impatience, fear, self-pity, and intolerance. Counteracting virtues, along with renewal of faith and a desire to spread cheer to others—not to be a burden—appear to be the purpose of the soul in meeting such physical Karma in this life. Cultivation of these virtues, and faith, appear to be of actual physical assistance in combating the inroads of multiple sclerosis and rebuilding the body.

Jesus told the multitudes, "Be ye therefore perfect, even as your Father which is in heaven is perfect."

The Edgar Cayce readings are excellent evidence of the truth that every defection from that perfection is reflected in our physical, mental, and spiritual bodies. Is that why pain purifies us? Why lack of knowledge goads us on to wisdom; why the deeds of the saints make us long for their virtue?

If pain does not purify us, perhaps it will come again and again, until we learn the lesson it is meant to teach. Every healing must be spiritual, else the sore is only covered up and will break open again. We can be obstinate in sin, but we can never be successful at it.

SPIRITUAL FACTORS FOR CONSIDERATION IN HEALTH AND HEALING

1. Consideration of the whole person—with Man as a spiritual being.
2. Mental/emotional conditions (Karma) can maintain health or bring about illnesses or accident. (Astrological aspects, too, can be involved here.)
3. There are no incurable diseases—only incurably stubborn minds and bodies.
4. Some people can only face the reality of their past errors by having their noses rubbed in it, so to speak. The Karmic situations noted in the multiple sclerosis cases are good examples of this.
5. Serious diseases require serious changes in attitude by the patient—faith, acceptance, optimism, cooperation, etc.

6. Dominant/responsive relationships between doctor, patient, and others are extremely important. In order for a patient to respond favorably to treatment and therapy there must be a mutual acceptance and respect. (Again the "I—Thou" concept in practice.) This can hold true especially for surgical cases and long-term patient/therapist relationships.

7. Positive/negative attitudes of doctors, nurses, and family can strongly affect a patient even though the patient is unconscious.

8. The above holds true also in maternity cases and even for the newborn child.

9. All treatment and therapy should be directed toward bringing about normal body balances.

10. All healing—as in the gift of life itself—comes from the Creator.

11. No man or woman should ever call himself a healer. Individuals can only be channels for healing.

12. Spiritual healing, seemingly miraculous, does happen. (In medical terminology this is usually referred to as "spontaneous remission.")

13. To die in the earth is to be reborn on the other side. For life goes on both there and here.

14. Prayers for the sick as well as prayers *by* the sick are very important. (And the prayer must be, "Let *Thy* will be done." One should not pray that another person be made well, but rather that healing be accomplished according to God's will in the matter. For some, death may be the healing!)

15. *Healing affirmation* (repeat several times in relaxed state): "Father God, I will the life force to flow, through each cell of my being—throughout the entire day—healing, regenerating this entire form and spirit."

HEALING APPROACHES FOUND IN THE READINGS

Practically every type of healing practice known to man was prescribed at one time or another in the readings. Additionally, techniques and applications were prescribed that seem to have been created for the individual's condition alone. Patients were sent to medical doctors and surgeons, chiropractors and osteopaths, naturopaths and naporapaths, physical therapists and masseurs, pharmacologists and herbalists.

The treatments advised many times over seem to revolve mainly around the following (in addition to the staple advice concerning attitudes, emotions, and prayer):

1. Proper diet—often cleansing diets.
2. Water intake—seven to eight glasses a day.
3. Regular exercise—proper circulation.
4. Proper eliminations and release of toxins (colonic irrigations were recommended for all).
5. Castor oil packs (used externally, on the abdomen, primarily), epsom salt packs, Glyco-thymoline packs, hot salt packs, etc.
6. Massage—spinal oil rubs.
7. Herbs, tonics, inhalants—in great variety.
8. Vibrational therapy—color, sound, music, electrical appliances.
9. Spinal manipulation and proper alignment was recommended in most of the physical readings.

Repeated emphasis was placed on proper body balances and balanced activities. Moderation in all things and recommendations to achieve balance was customarily given for the following:

1. Diet and food combinations.
2. Proper assimilation and utilization of foods.
3. The cerebrospinal and autonomic nervous system spinal manipulation recommended).
4. The endocrine system (herb tonics).
5. Liver/kidney activity (acid/alkaline)—cleansing diets and castor oil packs recommended.
6. Elimination and excretion of waste substances and toxins.

7. Circulation of blood and lymph (exercise, massage, hydrotherapy recommended).

Finally, there is the reminder that the body, if properly attended and atuned, has the potential to regenerate itself in seven years—not overnight, but in seven years. Patience, persistence, and the other disciplines must become part of our daily way of life if health and healing as desired are to become a part of the Ideal and Purposes in life.

Go slow; or make haste slowly. Be patient with self and with others. Do not work self into a state of overanxiety at the changes that will be found, or attempt to use up the strength and vitality mentally and physically to gain or maintain those balances that once were held in relationships to these; for these will come in their normal time. Forget not the source of thine inspiration in self, for they must be in the God of life, of truth, of hope, of love. (480–11)

Chapter X

Love and Forgiveness

Love ye one another and thus fulfill the law of God, for God is love. (524-1)

The Cayce readings indicate over and again that as individuals we are no closer to the kingdom of heaven than our ability to love and forgive the person we have hated the most or who in turn has despised us or hurt us the most—physically/mentally/emotionally—in this or other lifetimes.

For if ye have gained the entire world and yet have not learned love—ye have learned nothing, ye have gained nothing. (See Chapter I, p. 18 #3744-4)

Again, the Master's admonition of "Whatsoever you do unto the least of these thy brethren . . ." is applicable here in that what we do to others, even in thought, we do to ourselves. As we hate others, we hate ourselves, and the hatred is eventually returned as it has been sown.

For, if ye *hate* thy brother, what will it profit thee to gain the whole world? And the brother doesn't mean the son of thy mother! It may be the one that's the furthest from thee, and the greatest persecutor of thine own people! Hate brings that which is irritating especially to those that are creative in other directions. (1727-1)

Until ye can see in each person that ye meet, though in error he may be, his special worth—*that ye would worship in thy Lord,* ye have not even begun to find the meaning of Brotherhood. (1402-2)

Q: Describe the difference between fellowship and brotherhood.
A: One to God, the other (brotherhood) to man. (262-22)

Q: Can brotherhood exist among men without true fellowship?
A: Fellowship is, first, brotherhood. A pattern of—or a shadow of—what fellowship is; for, *as has been given, all one sees manifest in a material world is but a reflection or a shadow of the real or the spiritual life.* Brotherhood, then, is an expression (in the earth) of the fellowship that exists in the SPIRITUAL life. (262-23)

Basic to any discussion of love there must be a positive affirmative attitude regarding these initial statements. (At present can you agree with them?) Regardless of how our inner emotions may rankle at the concept of every other human actually *being* an expression of God in the earth, the readings indicate that this is truth. Consider the following two readings along with your own past and present attitudes related to them. Do your thoughts and emotions agree in each case?

Think not more highly of thyself than ye ought—for ye have not begun to think straight until ye are able to see in the life of those whom ye utterly dislike something ye would worship in thy Maker. For each soul-entity in the earth, with life, whether of this or that shade or color, or whether this or that disfigurement of body or mind, is in the earth by the grace of God. (For He has not willed that any soul should perish, and has thus prepared a way of escape.) And ye, as His servant, as the child of the Living God, are given the opportunity to contribute to the welfare of any whom ye even considered not quite on a par with thy opportunity. (3575-2)

Not that thine experience . . . may be entirely different from that of thine next door neighbor, but find not fault in thine friend nor in thine enemy; for, hath not He, the Father, allowed the tares and the wheat to grow up together? Be not as one that would tell the Father, the Creator, as to who the tares are—or as to when such a tare should be rooted up. Be thou rather found in the way *of blooming,* of bringing forth fruit worthy of a son that has been endowed with the privileges of manifesting the spirit that He has shed abroad in the earth through the gift to the world of the Babe in Bethlehem. (440–4)

LOVE IS GOD'S LAW

For the error that man makes is the more oft against himself than making for the breaking of law as related to Divine influence in the experience. *For, love is law —law is love, in its essence. And with the breaking of the law is the making of the necessity for atonement and forgiveness,* in that which may take away error to or (from) what has been brought in the experience of the individual.

Hence the shedding of the blood in the *man* Jesus made for the atoning for *all* men, *through making Himself in at-onement with the law and with love. For, through love was brought the desire to make self and His brother in at-onement. Hence in the atoning or shedding of (His) blood comes the redemption to man, through that which may make for his* (man's) *at-onement with Him.* (262–45)

As noted previously, we can possess only that which we freely give, so that in order to become love, or more Godlike (All-Giving), we must give that which is God. (Again, Love.) *The essential key to this is Forgiveness.* In our opinion forgiveness and love are inseparable within the creative scheme of the soul's experience. The readings indicate that God has always, already forgiven us for whatever errors we commit, and while we must eventually meet whatever we have sown, the forgiveness lies within self. Our greatest problem is that we have not forgiven or will not forgive self! (Perhaps forgiveness is "love grown up"?)

Here the dominant/responsive role is in evidence. God in the dominant role has forgiven us—as a "love/risk" decision. The individual, being in the responsive role, can either accept or reject that Love, but it can be accepted *only* by forgiving self. Thus we become a co-creator or co-forgiver with God—at one with God's Will, which is forgiveness. However, one can forgive self only *as* one forgives others!

> Remember in thy relationships to others—the RULE does not alter. Ye are forgiven from on High as ye forgive others. (2409–1)

Note the emphasis once more on application. Forgiveness must be *applied* in order to take effect!

Again, the responsive party holds the key role in the relationship (even within self) in that only by being open to and living up to the Christ Consciousness or God force within can the cleansing or healing, or atonement, take place.

> Will ye pray, will ye ask God and Christ to forgive thee? Will ye forgive others? *For it is only as ye forgive* that even the Saviour, the Christ, *is able to forgive thee.* But if ye forgive, it will be doubled to thee in thy abilities, in thy actvities, in thy improvements. (3124)

Or, as we've noted before, the only unforgivable sin mentioned in the Bible is the denial of the Holy Spirit or Christ Consciousness, for as the readings have stated, our free will allows us to defy even God Himself, even His Love, even His Forgiveness. In this manner there is no eternal damnation, no hell or purgatory, other than in self's unwillingness to forgive self—in self's willfulness in serving self rather than God's Will. This would seem to be the original sin, and even though (as children) we may have been baptized and cleansed in potential before the eyes of the Lord, our old habit patterns later tend to lead us astray!

Q: Where am I falling short?
A: *Whom am I, that should speak against any fault in any soul?* Seek rather to find the fault from thine own inner self, and He (the Christ) will guide thee aright. So spake He to those that asked of Him, and so speaks He to those that seek. (262–51)

The above reading is the only instance the writer has found to date where the sleeping Cayce refers to himself in first-person singular.

If you forgive not those who have in any manner caused the disturbance or distress, how may ye expect thy heavenly Father to forgive you of thy trespasses, of thy shortcomings? (1532–1)

The entity is inclined toward benevolence, inclined to forgive and yet not forget too easily. Oft the entity makes promises to self and because of attributes of others never quite meets the obligation in self. (3298–1)

All will remember how He said, as He took the little child, *Unless ye become as a little child, ye shall in no wise enter in!* Unless you become as open-minded, unless you can get mad and fight and then forgive and forget. . . . For it is the nature of man to fight, while it is the nature of God to forgive. (3395–3)

(Blindness: Prenatal: Karmic) While conditions may appear as hopeless in the present, know there is forgiveness. Even as the body-mind may forgive others, so may the body here be forgiven. So may it soak through those promises of the All-Creative forces for help, yes; help in a physical as well as in a mental matter. (3504–1)

(Reconciliation, between wife and husband) Yes, this can be—if there is ever the offering to forgive and forget. Don't forgive and say, "I'll remember it—I forgive you, but I'll keep on remembering it." If you do, you'd better not try. (5001–1)

Q: Explain why the Master in many cases forgave sins?
A: Sins are of commission and omission, sins of commission were forgiven, while sins of omission were called to mind—even by the Master. (281–2)

There is prepared for each soul a way of escape. *For not of self alone may one meet self;* but in not only the forgiveness in self but in the abilities of expressing self that others may forgive also. (1096–1)

How many times should we forgive? How many times have we *been* forgiven? The Bible (Matthew 18:21, 22) says we should forgive 70 times 7. (The George Lamsa translation from the original Aramaic texts states it as 70 times 77!) This is really saying that forgiveness should be nonending—as it is with God's forgiveness of us. We are always forgiven, as noted before, though we have to pay the price for error. Again, our most difficult problem is that of forgiving self through forgiveness of others. (And this may well be part of the original sin, too!) We may reach the point of forgiving all the Hitlers and Neros of history—even those who have personally wronged us—but still we are faced with forgiving self.

Possibly the only way we can finally effect such a change *is through service to others.* At least this is the author's opinion. For as the readings indicate, "No man enters the kingdom of Heaven except on the arm of someone he has aided somewhere in the past." And, it has always seemed to me that when the moment comes for the Last Judgment—the very last soul to make it into the Kingdom will come on the arm of the Master—our Elder Brother—the Christ.

Who gains by being forgiven and by forgiving? The one that forgives is lord even of him *that he forgives.* (585–2)

Let the mind ever be in thee as was in Him as He offered Himself up: "Father forgive them—they know not what they do. Father it is finished—I come to thee. Give Thou thy servant that glory which Thou has promised." (5759–13)

In what manner shall we be of service? Consider the following—with its emphasis on Joy:

Be joyous in the service, *even as He was joyous in the service,* even as He was joyous in the life that He led as the man—Jesus.

Come sing a joyous song unto the Lord for the good that has been brought into thine experience through the service that thou renderest in His name. Make a joyous noise unto the Lord, for His ways are the joyous life.

Keep the heart singing. *Look not upon the service to Him as being duty; rather as the privilege to show forth in thine life, thine experience, the blessings that have been and that may be thine in an opportunity of service to thy fellow man.*

And know ye that unless the experience is thine own to thine own soul (applied) it is only theory. (473–1)

All of our initial expressions of love may not bring about this immediate inner response of joy however, try as we may. If so, give "Loving indifference" a try:

Then only in *LOVING INDIFFERENCE* may the condition be met. What, say ye, is loving indifference? Acting as if it had not been—disregarding—as if it were not. Not animosity—not anger. (1402–2)

(Again: "It doesn't matter—because it doesn't matter.")

Also, we do not conclude that the tearing loose from self's selfish attainments will be accomplished totally without pain and suffering, even thou as individuals we may be properly dedicated in love, service and forgiveness.

For as the individual entity or soul becomes the more sensitive to the attunement of itself with Divinity, the more the hurt will be. (1158–5)

Know this, learn this well. God is mindful of thee and will not allow thee to suffer beyond that ye are able to bear in thy body-mind, that ye may prepare the soul for the closer walk with Him. (5348–1)

We are reminded in the Bible of the hurts and sufferings within even that most purposeful of individuals, when the Master said: "O Jerusalem, Jerusalem—how often I wanted to gather your children, just as a hen gathers her chickens under her wings, and yet you would not!" (Matthew 23:37) "Again, I have many other things to tell you, but you cannot bear them now." (John 16:12) And the Bible's shortest, most eloquent passage: "Jesus wept."

OTHER THOUGHTS ON LOVE

For one can only hurt that which one loves. (3285–2)

Similarly, one can only *be* hurt or emotionally upset by that which one loves—even if that something is one's own unconscious desire for attention, acclaim, control or possession. (Here the "two-edged sword" concept applies once more—in that hurting for others is one thing and one side of it; hurting for self is that other ragged edge!)

Possibly one of the greatest flaws in the American public educational system has been in not considering Love as a necessary part of the curriculum. All too often love has been equated wholly with sex—which it should not be, as noted by previous readings—and that, too, has been educationally avoided with equally unfortunate results. (Having taught classes in biology, health/hygiene, and sex education, I feel that I know of what I speak.) In my opinion, if all aspects of Love, aside from sexuality, had been served to our nation's youth as applied courses from kindergarten through college over the past two hundred years, we would not now be experiencing many of the problems we have in our social, political and racial relationships. But this is what we have sown as a nation. Consequently, what we are presently experiencing as human love often falls short of perfection, or permanence—possibly because we sense it or apply it only in bits and pieces, without having been taught to perceive the totality.

Dr. Lindsay Jacob has suggested that "Love is something you do *with* someone—not *to* someone." This is very true of sensual or erotic love, but still all too often we confuse passion or sexual fulfillment with love and loving while disregarding the spiritual implications of such acts and relationships.

In short, if physical lovemaking is not accomplished "with" someone, in a mutually agreeable, mutually responsive spiritually creative manner, then invariably one or both parties will be found to be playing ego/power/control games or otherwise accomplishing what essentially amounts to using someone else's body for purposes of masturbation.

So in pursuing concepts of these bits and pieces of Love's totality, or the "nuts and bolts" of love, as Dr. Jacob has puckishly phrased it (from out of his background in Freudian analysis), perhaps we should suggest to ourselves just what love is or what it is not. (Most of these are touched upon in the readings, while some are from other sources.)

LOVE IS NOT

Love is not being possessive or jealous.
(Friends, mates, even one's children, are not to be regarded as "property.")

Love is not *"business"*—it should not be, "I'll love you *if*—" (Keeping strings attached comes from fear or safety-seeking positions within a relationship, of course.)

Love is not saying, "After all I've done for you!" (For then one can ask in return "So why did you do it?")

Love is not saying, "How could you do this *to me?"* (Probably because they deservedly had it coming to them?)

Love is not demanding more than another can freely give.

Love is not feeling superior to any other being.

Love is not "sitting in judgment."

Yes, we have the records here of this entity now known as or called (3663). Not all of these are pretty, if they were judged by the standards of morality, or beauty, of today—or in any period—*but who is to judge his fellowman?*

Not all of the activities of the entity in the present experience are without question, but who is to question? For the entity must, as must each entity, give an account for the deeds done in the body. *To whom must it give the account? To the God-force within itself!* And think—when it is hate and malice, jealousy and selfishness—what a poor, miserable soul has to bring, as a body, before the Lord its King! (3663–1)

An entity, an individual who desires to reform the whole world and every individual with whom he comes in contact. At present it is not egotism. It is a body-mind with a vision. The desire is to do this through political, through economic situations, *but who made thee to be a judge of thy fellowman?* (5249–1)

How often are we inclined to prejudge others on the basis of first impressions, hearsay, or categorizing individuals because of their age, race, sex, nationality, or even their hairstyle?

Then be not too quick on thy judgments of others. Put thyself in their place, in thy mind, before ye pass judgment on others. (1510-1)

But judgments of morality, judgments of activity through those periods (of the past) would not be in the same class as in the present. Though truth and morality is ever the same, the outward application of same has changed as man's application of ideals as related to same has changed. (2772-5)

Ye have the ability to judge things. It is well to judge things—it is bad to judge yourself or your fellowman. Whatever the activities may be, whether pertaining to a washing machine or a flying machine, it is well to judge its abilities to serve man. For the injunction to man is to subdue the earth. Then all the powers of creation are in the hands of man, and ye are a very good one to handle much of these—but know that these abilities are lent thee by a divine power. Who made thee lord of any soul? (3544)

The readings point out that each of us is unique, with individual soul purposes, and we are not to judge, condemn, or deter another soul from its fruition. This is the parable of the mustard seed. Jesus told the Diciples of this when they tried to stop Him from going to Jerusalem. His explanation was that it was for this reason He came into the earth—to fulfill His purpose, as a seed of any nature, expressing God's will according to His time and place and manner.

How many different kinds of seeds are in the earth? How many varieties are there of birds and fishes? Still we fall into the trap of demanding conformity from our children and ourselves. How often have we heard the refrains, "Why don't you get good grades like so-and-so?" "Why aren't you on the first team?" "Why can't you behave like so-and-so down the block?" and so on. To this we would ask, "Do you go out in the garden and start kicking your rosebushes because they don't give you bananas?"

LOVE IS NOT BEING INTOLERANT OF SELF

For often we find here and there, as within this entity, *unusual* aspects. *For the entity is more tolerant with others than with self;* (while) the usual, of course, is to excuse self and blame others.

This produces within the entity a great deal of latent abilities. Yet there must never be any more of self-condemnation than condemning of others. (1744–1)

LOVE IS NOT CONDEMNING SELF

There are evidences of unusual abilities with this body —if once removed (from it) the feelings of inferiority, or of self-condemnation. (2402–1)

Condemn not self, condemn not others. (2522–1)

Q: Why is the thought always with me to kill myself? A: *Self-condemnation.* For (there is within self), *not enough of that seeking to manifest God's will.* . . . When this thought (of self-destruction) occurs, let thy prayer be . . . "Lord, here am I—thine! Use me in those ways and manners as Thou seest—that I may ever glorify Thee!" (2540–1)

One who has often suffered self-condemnation through the lack of exercising that which it knew to be the correct thing to do, or have done at the time. (The Sin of Omission) (4562–2)

Do not condemn others! *Do not* condemn self! Self-condemnation for that which is past, that which cannot be rectified, is but to heap reproach upon self. Reproach not self *nor* others. . . . Let thy yeas be yeas, and thy nays be nays. *Learn when to say yea, and when to say nay!* (5469-1)

LOVE IS NOT JUSTIFYING SELF

. . . *Know that if and when the Lord is with thee, ye are already in the great majority!* Ye are then glorifying the Lord—not attempting to justifying self. *For justifying self is blaming someone else.* (2803-2)

LOVE IS NOT BEING A DOORMAT!

To allow another to take advantage of self or a situation is to do them a disservice, say the readings.

To be sure, patience, long-suffering and endurance are in their respective manners urges that would lead to virtues, but they cease to be a virtue when the individual entity allows self merely to be imposed upon, and to take second place merely because someone else, of a more aggressive nature, imposes. . . . (3029-1)

LOVE IS NOT BEING PERMISSIVE!

Even Jesus chased the money changers from the temple. In our present "permissive society" we see many of the fruits of parents who have reared their children out of fear or "safety-seeking" positions. To allow selfish, willful children free rein is to bring forth the potential of a destructively arrogant, indolent and resentful, self-oriented generation. How it will all come out remains to be seen.

LOVE IS

Love is seeing God in all that exists.

Love is being a light of love to others.
For flowers will love the entity, as the entity loves the

flowers. Very few would ever find it in themselves to wither while about or on this body. (5122–1)

Love is giving—completely—with no strings attached, with no need or expectation of reciprocation. (For love of sufficient unto love—and virtue should be its only needed reward.)

Love is putting "others first."

Love is allowing others complete freedom to be themselves.

Love is accepting others as they are—not as how we would like them to be.

Love is being respectful of others' thoughts and privacy. (And their time, too.)

Love is sharing—"Filling the other's cup."

Love is attempting to give what best is needed by another individual. (Saying or doing the right thing at the right time and place.)

Love is praying that God's Will be done through others—even if it hurts you in the outcome.

Love is accepting the fact that others may hate you for doing (risking) what you know is right and proper.

Love is being able to stand knowing the truth about yourself—and others.

Love is being able to bear whatever you have asked for. (For example, if one really asks for another's personal opinion about self, or the actuality of a situation and then cannot stand the answer or ends up hating or resenting the other for being honest, then better never to have asked.)

Love is *being* God's Will in the earth. (Being true to self and self's *inner guidance—knowing that one can and should be a channel for the Creative Force—remembering that it was said even of Him, "Can any good thing come out of Nazareth?"*)

LOVE IS BEING OF SERVICE

For it is not by change that any individual soul enters but that God hath need of thee at this time. They then who begin to pity themselves or wonder what it is all about, lose the real purpose of Love; that ye may make manifest the love He hath chosen to give thee. (5149–1)

In every way and manner present self and self's service for the service's sake, and not for self's sake, see? (288–16)

LOVE IS BEING A GOOD EXAMPLE FOR THE CHILDREN OF THE EARTH

LOVE IS BEING ABLE TO STAND UP AND SPEAK OUT FOR WHAT ONE FIRMLY BELIEVES IN

True, one must become selfless, but to have knowledge and withhold same from others, is not always best. . . .

Be willing ever, to give account of the reason for the faith that lies within—don't be afraid to speak of same. (2775–1)

LOVE IS BEING HUMBLE

The entity often through other influences, as we shall see, rather belittle's self's abilities. Humbleness is well; *but "who lighteth the candle and putteth it under a bushel?"* (1315–2)

Humbleness does not mean, then, degrading nor becoming discouraged when self has been refused that which according to the principles of self is debased by those that SHOULD be, are in the position to be, helpful experiences in the affairs of the entity. (1466–3)

LOVE IS HAVING FAITH AND TRUST

And when ye trust in Him ye are sure—and need never be afraid of the material things. For, does He not feed the birds of the air? Does He not give the color to the lily, the incense to the violet?

How much more is that as may be in His very presence, *if ye apply self* to become worthy of acceptance in His home. (333–1)

Confidence, then, is of the material or of the physical sense—while *faith* is an attribute of the soul and spiritual body. (281–10)

Love is being able to admit to self and others that you were wrong. (And with sincerity.)

Love is being sorry enough to never want to do wrong again.

Love is going to someone you've wronged and truly asking forgiveness. (The readings are very positive toward the need and effectiveness of such aspects of confession and also for confessional prayer. Truly to be sorry and attempt making restitution can even work in the case of prayers for the dead—where the offended party is beyond telephone, mail, or face-to-face contact. Yet all are worthwhile approaches—so state the readings!)

Also, love is so being that others will find us easy *to* forgive! (We should be able to state simply and honestly, "I was wrong, I'm sorry. Please forgive me—I'll try to make up for it in whatever way you feel is agreeable.")

Last though not least, by any means:

LOVE IS—

PATIENCE—PATIENCE—PATIENCE

Q: Any other advice that will be of help at this time?
A: Much might be said, *but if there is the looking within so much more may be received than could otherwise be referred to here.*

The Lord bless thee, the Lord keep thee in thy purposes, in thy desires.

Faint not because of disagreements or disappointments. *Sow the Seed of Truth; as ye are directed by the God-Force within;* then have the *patience* to leave the increase to the Giver of all good and perfect gifts.

Ye do not plant a seed and constantly scratch it up to see what has happened—but you do nourish it, you do water it, you do feed it in the way that is in keeping with the NATURE of that you are seeking to gain from same.

You do not sow salt upon those things that need iron. You do not give iron to those that need soda. You do not give this, that, or the other to those that need something else.

But as He is the water of life, as He is the bread of life—*so in all thy undertakings, ye water, ye nourish, ye feed; and leave the results to thy God!* (1151–12)

Then, (in living, in being, in applying these concepts), show forth *the fruits of the spirit.* What are these? Faith, hope, patience, long-suffering, kindness, gentleness, brotherly love (mercy)—*these be those over which so many stumble;* yet they are the very voices, yea the very morning sun's light in which the entity has caught that vision of the NEW AGE, the new understanding,

Recommended Reading

A Search for God, Books I and II, and *A Handbook for Group Study*, Virginia Beach, Va., A.R.E. Press, 1942, 1957.

Boehme, Jacob, *Personal Christianity*. New York, Frederick Ungar.

Bro, Harmon H., *Edgar Cayce on Religion & Psychic Experience*. New York, Paperback Library, 1970.

Buber, Martin, *I and Thou*. New York, Scribners, 1958.

Cayce, Hugh Lynn, *Venture Inward*. New York, Harper & Row, 1964.

Cerminara, Gina, *Many Mansions*. New York, W. Sloan Associates, 1950.

Durant, Will, *The Story of Philosophy*. New York, Simon & Schuster, 1926; New York, Pocket Library, 1954.

Fromm, Erich, *The Art of Loving*. New York, Harper & Row, 1956.

Furst, Jeffrey, *Edgar Cayce's Story of Jesus*. New York, Coward-McCann, 1969.

Gibran, Kahlil, *The Prophet*. New York, Alfred A. Knopf, 1961.

Goldsmith, Joel, *The Thunder of Silence*. New York, Harper & Row, 1961.

Head, Joseph, and Cranston, S. L., *Reincarnation: An East-West Anthology*. New York, Julian Press, 1961.

James, William, *The Varieties of Religious Experience.* New York, Mentor Books, 1958.

Jung, C. G., *Memories, Dreams, Reflections.* New York, Vintage Books, 1965.

Kelsey, Morton T., *Dreams: The Dark Speech of the Spirit.* New York, Doubleday, 1968.

Kidd, Worth, *Edgar Cayce and Group Dynamics.* Virginia Beach, Va., A.R.E. Press, 1971.

Maltz, Maxwell, *Psycho-Cybernetics.* Englewood Cliffs, N.J., Prentice-Hall, 1960.

Martin, P. W., *Experiment in Depth.* London, Routledge & Kegan Paul, 1955.

Sorokin, Pitirim, *Forms and Techniques of Altruistic & Spiritual Growth.* Boston, Beacon Press, 1954.

Starcke, Walter, *The Ultimate Revolution.* New York, Harper & Row, 1969.

Wilhelm, Richard, and Jung, Carl, *The Secret of the Golden Flower.* New York, Harcourt, Brace & World, 1962.

Woodward, Mary Ann, *Edgar Cayce's Story of Karma.* New York, Coward-McCann, 1971.

Yogananda, Paramahansa, *Autobiography of a Yogi.* Los Angeles, Self-Realization Fellowship, 1946.

Yutang, Lin, *The Importance of Living.* New York, John Day, 1937.